Questions of Jurisdiction and Admissibility before International Courts

This examination of the jurisdiction of international courts and the admissibility of cases before them analyses jurisdictional and admissibility rules in light of the roles assumed by international courts in international life and in light of the roles that jurisdictional and admissibility rules play in promoting the effectiveness and legitimacy of international courts. The theory pursued views jurisdiction as a form of delegation of power (the power to exercise judicial power and decide on the interpretation and application of the law) and regards admissibility as a framework for deciding upon the propriety of exercising such power. On the basis of this theoretical framework, the author critically evaluates the exercise of judicial discretion in the existing case law of a variety of international courts, distinguishing between the category-based case selection implicit in jurisdictional rules and the case-by-case analysis and selection implicit in rules on admissibility.

YUVAL SHANY is the Hersch Lauterpacht Chair in International Law at the Law Faculty of the Hebrew University of Jerusalem. He is also a member of the UN Human Rights Committee.

Recent books in the Hersch Lauterpacht Memorial Lecture Series

Yuval Shany *Questions of Jurisdiction and Admissibility before International Courts*

W. Michael Reisman and Christina Skinner *Fraudulent Evidence before Public International Tribunals: The Dirty Stories of International Law*

Andrés Rigo Sureda *Investment Treaty Arbitration: Judging Under Uncertainty*

Ralph Zacklin *The United Nations Secretariat and the Use of Force in a Unipolar World: Power v. Principle*

John H. Jackson *Sovereignty, the WTO, and Changing Fundamentals of International Law*

Jan Paulsson *Denial of Justice in International Law*

Francisco Orrego Vicuna *International Dispute Settlement in an Evolving Global Society: Constitutionalization, Accessibility, Privatization*

Martti Koskenniemi *The Gentle Civilizer of Nations: The Rise and Fall of International Law 1870–1960*

Thomas M. Franck *Recourse to Force: State Action against Threats and Armed Attacks*

Antonio Cassese *Self-Determination of Peoples: A Legal Reappraisal*

Questions of Jurisdiction and Admissibility before International Courts

YUVAL SHANY

CAMBRIDGE
UNIVERSITY PRESS

CAMBRIDGE
UNIVERSITY PRESS

University Printing House, Cambridge CB2 8BS, United Kingdom

Cambridge University Press is part of the University of Cambridge.

It furthers the University's mission by disseminating knowledge in the pursuit of education, learning and research at the highest international levels of excellence.

www.cambridge.org
Information on this title: www.cambridge.org/9781107038790

First published 2016

A catalogue record for this publication is available from the British Library

Library of Congress Cataloguing in Publication Data
Shany, Yuval, author.
Questions of jurisdiction and admissibility before international courts / Yuval Shany.
pages cm. – (Hersch lauterpacht memorial lectures ; 22)
ISBN 978-1-107-03879-0 (hardback)
1. International courts. 2. Jurisdiction (International law) 3. Admissable evidence. I. Title.
KZ6265.S53 2016
341.5′5–dc23
2015032291

ISBN 978-1-107-03879-0 Hardback

Contents

Preface

This book is based on a series of lectures delivered in the Lauterpacht Centre for International Law at the University of Cambridge during the spring of 2012 as part of the Sir Hersch Lauterpacht Memorial Lecture Series. The invitation to deliver the lecture series was particularly meaningful and moving for me, since I have been very fortunate to hold the Hersch Lauterpacht Chair in Public International Law at my home university – the Hebrew University of Jerusalem, and I was very pleased and honoured to have been given the opportunity to be associated with the prestigious lecture series bearing the name of this giant of public international law. I am thus extremely grateful to the organizers of the lecture series for inviting me to speak therein, and I am in particular indebted to Professor James Crawford, the then director of the Centre, and to Sir Eli Lauterpacht, who opened the lecture series and has been a constant source of support and inspiration.

I am also very grateful to the Cambridge University Press team, and in particular to Mr. Richard Woodham and to Ms Finola O'Sullivan, who encouraged me to develop the lecture to a book and patiently waited for the manuscript. I also thank Mr Shaul Vardi, for his valuable assistance in style editing, and Ms Noa Schreuer, for her hard work on the book's footnotes and Mr. Philip Alexander, who managed the editing process on behalf of Cambridge University Press.

Finally, I am grateful to my family for all their love and support. Without their continuous backing, especially that of my wife Merav, I would not have been able to offer the Lauterpacht lectures or prepare this manuscript for print.

Introduction

The focus of inquiry

This book studies the role that legal rules on jurisdiction and admissibility play in the life and operation of international courts. I will argue that jurisdictional rules define the legal powers of courts and that admissibility rules define their ability to refrain from exercising legal power. Accordingly, the underlying subject of this book is the legal power that international courts can exercise in the international realm. Of course, legal powers are not the only type of power that courts may exercise, courts also exert political influence and moral authority, and contribute to shaping the legal culture of the various constituencies with which they interact.[1] Nevertheless, legal powers are central to the operation of international courts. Not only do legal powers constitute the most dominant or quintessential set of powers exercised by international courts; legal powers also delineate and confer legitimacy upon the other powers wielded by international courts, thereby facilitating and controlling all aspects of their operation.

Arguably, the most important consequence of the application by international courts of the rules on jurisdiction and admissibility governing their legal powers is case selection. Jurisdictional and admissibility rules introduce legal criteria that provide an answer to

[1] See e.g. Karen J Alter, 'The European Court's Political Power' (1996) 19 *West European Politics* 458; Sally Engle Merry, *Colonizing Hawai'i: The Cultural Power of Law* (Princeton, NJ: Princeton University Press, 2000), pp. 17–18; Jack Wade Nowlin, 'Judicial Moral Expertise and Real-World Constraints on Judicial Moral Reasoning', in Christopher Wolfe (ed.), *That Eminent Tribunal: Judicial Supremacy and the Constitution* (Princeton, NJ: Princeton University Press, 2004), p. 118.

the question whether international courts can or should adjudicate specific international disputes. Case selection thus mediates the influence that international courts exert on the world of international law and international relations. The centrality of case selection for understanding and appreciating the scope of international judicial power underlies my decision to focus my attention in this book almost exclusively on the implications of jurisdiction and admissibility rules for case selection. I will therefore allude here only in passing to other meanings of the term 'jurisdiction', which are sometimes employed in the literature on international adjudication to refer to aspects of legal power other than case selection such as the judicial power to issue specific remedies or adopt certain interim measures.[2]

Outline

The book adopts the following thematic structure: Part I investigates from a primarily theoretical perspective the concepts of jurisdiction and admissibility and their contribution to the life and operation of international courts. My main claim in this regard is that jurisdiction and admissibility can be understood as a form of delegated authority afforded to international courts to exercise adjudicative powers and/or to refrain from doing so. Parts II and III, which constitute the main parts of this book, then examine the actual application by international courts of rules on jurisdiction and admissibility (Part II focuses on rules of jurisdiction and Part III on rules of admissibility). The analysis I offer in both of these parts is as much prescriptive as descriptive. My main claim in this regard is that a critical assessment of the relevant practice and literature on questions of jurisdiction

[2] Some surprising links can be found between different meanings of the term 'jurisdiction'. E.g. the broad power of the ICJ to entertain advisory opinion (jurisdiction to adjudicate) may be explained in part by reference to the non-binding effect of the decision (jurisdiction to prescribe), and the Court's inability to issue any remedies (remedial jurisdiction). *Interpretation of Peace Treaties with Bulgaria, Hungary and Romania* (first phase), 1950 ICJ 65, 71 ('The consent of States, parties to a dispute, is the basis of the Court's jurisdiction in contentious cases. The situation is different concerning advisory proceedings even where the Request for an Opinion relates to a legal question actually pending between States. The Court's reply is only of an advisory character: as such, it has no binding force. It follows that no State, whether a Member of the United Nations or not, can prevent the giving of an Advisory Opinion which the United Nations considers to be desirable in order to obtain enlightenment as to the course of action it should take').

and admissibility reveals numerous inconsistencies, thereby highlighting the absence of a coherent theory on jurisdiction and admissibility and their role in international adjudication. The functional approach I advance in this book has, I believe, the potential to address many of the shortcomings found in the existing practice and literature and to explain in coherent terms the exercise of judicial power.

Part I

The concept of jurisdiction and admissibility in international adjudication

1

Jurisdiction as a policy tool

A functional approach to jurisdiction and admissibility

The approach I present in this book to the study of rules on jurisdiction and admissibility and their contribution to the operation of international courts is primarily functional (or instrumental) in nature, and places jurisdictional and admissibility rules in the context of the variety of functions international courts and tribunals serve in the life of the international community (or international society). Such functions include: (1) conflict resolution or, more broadly, advancing the solution and/or facilitating the management of policy problems occupying states, international organizations and other relevant actors; and (2) interpretation of relevant legal norms and their application to concrete factual situations, thereby potentially contributing to the development of international law norms, strengthening their centrality in international relations and inculcating the notion of the rule of law at the international level.[1]

More generally, international courts can also be understood as policy instruments in the hands of two principal sets of constituencies: (1) their mandate providers – that is, the states and international organizations that establish international courts, fund and support their operation, and who may ultimately decide to shut down and dissolve them; and (2) the parties to any specific dispute,

[1] For a discussion of the functions of international courts, see Armin von Bogdandy and Ingo Venzke, 'On the Functions of International Courts: An Appraisal in Light of Their Burgeoning Public Authority' (2013) 26 *Leiden Journal of International Law* 49; Yuval Shany, *Assessing the Effectiveness of International Courts* (New York: Oxford University Press, 2014), pp. 37–48.

who may choose to submit their differences to adjudication before an international court. The decision by both sets of constituencies to create an international court or to utilize it in any specific case can be explained in policy terms by the perceived functional utility of adjudication in addressing policy problems confronting international actors. One functional utility of adjudication is legitimization, and this may explain the choice of adjudication over other problem-solving alternatives. The establishment and activation of international courts, which exercise legal powers in an independent and impartial manner and reach their decisions through a process, which is generally perceived as fair and professional, can be understood as a method by which international actors bolster and legitimize specific dispute-resolution outcomes, as well as, more broadly, the governance of the international legal regimes to which they belong.[2]

From this functional perspective, one may view the establishment of international courts, the conferral of jurisdiction upon them and their actual activation in concrete cases as means to an end: a way to advance the goals, interests and values of international actors belonging to relevant political communities or legal regimes. In this context, rules on jurisdiction typically serve as the method by which the mandate providers and disputing parties control the space reserved for the court's judicial operations and, consequently, the extent of its functional utility. Rules on admissibility, however, allow international courts to resist certain attempts to utilize them in a manner they consider improper or harmful to their own institutional interests or those of their constituencies.

The conferral of *ex ante* jurisdiction upon an international court, discussed in Part II of this book, reflects the choice of the mandate providers or potential parties to any given dispute to create conditions under which certain political, economic or societal interactions will take place under the shadow of international adjudication – that is, in a judicialized environment, where rights can be enforced before a court of law.[3] Such a judicialized environment stands in marked

[2] On the relationship between legitimacy and functional effectiveness, see Shany, 'Assessing the Effectiveness of International Courts', pp. 137–138.

[3] E.g., see Understanding on Rules and Procedures governing the Settlement of Disputes (Annex 2 of the WTO Agreement), 15 April 1994, art. 3(2), 1869 UNTS 401 (hereinafter 'DSU') ('The dispute settlement system of the WTO is a central element in providing security and predictability to the multilateral trading system. The members recognize that it serves to preserve the rights and obligations of the

contrast to the traditional state of affairs in international relations, where specific problems, including problems with conspicuous legal dimensions, have tended to be resolved (if at all) through diplomacy.[4] In the same vein, the actual activation of an international court's jurisdiction in any specific case (through unilateral seizing of the court or through reference by way of agreement of the parties) reflects a choice by one or more of the disputing parties to realize the potential offered by the legalized environment in which they operate and to opt for law-based problem solving through the process of adjudication.[5]

In both cases – the *ex ante* conferral of jurisdiction upon international courts and its *ex post* invocation – the scope of jurisdiction held and exercised by international courts is expected to correlate, by and large, to certain broadly held notions about the utility of adjudication, which are explored in the ensuing pages. Furthermore, the actual caseload of international courts is likely to reflect the beliefs and expectations of parties to litigation about the type of situations in which international courts may serve as useful tools for advancing law-based problem solving.

A similar functional analysis may be offered with regard to rules on admissibility. As Part III shows, the conferral upon an international court of the power to reject cases as inadmissible equips it with independent case-selection capabilities which may help it to protect its reputation and adjudicative functions. In addition, the actual dismissal of cases by international courts as non-admissible is indicative of judicial perceptions of the circumstances under which

members under the covered agreements, and to clarify the existing provisions of those agreements in accordance with customary rules of interpretation of public international law'); Security Council Resolution 827 (25 May 1993), preamble, UN Doc. S/RES/827 (1993) ('Convinced that in the particular circumstances of the former Yugoslavia the establishment as an ad hoc measure by the Council of an international tribunal and the prosecution of persons responsible for serious violations of international humanitarian law would enable this aim [bringing international criminals to justice] to be achieved and would contribute to the restoration and maintenance of peace').

4 See e.g. Bernardo Sepulveda-Amor, 'Opening Remarks', in Laurence Boisson de Chazournes, Marcelo G Kohen and Jorge E Vinuales (eds.), *Diplomatic and Judicial Means of Dispute Settlement* (Leiden: Martinus Nijhoff Publishers, 2013), p. 7.

5 See e.g. Patricia Rey Mallén, 'Landlocked For A Century, Bolivia Now Wants Access To The Sea, Asks Chile For Help', *International Business Times,* 14 June 2013 (alluding to Bolivian president Morales's decision to go to 'international courts and organizations, asking for the right of Bolivia to have its own way to the Pacific' as underlying the Bolivia-Chile ICJ case).

adjudication would be disruptive of the judicial function or undesirable for other reasons. For example, the International Court of Justice (ICJ) has in the past taken the position that adjudicating a case raising only hypothetical legal questions, without any practical consequences, is incompatible with the judicial function and should thus be resisted through designating the case as inadmissible.[6] This is reflective of a perception about the non-utility of adjudicating legal disputes without any real-life consequences, which can be said to stem from a particular view about the function of international courts in international life.

The granting of jurisdiction to international courts over a category of disputes or over any specific dispute does not, however, imply that judicial settlement is always regarded by the relevant mandate providers or disputing parties as the only suitable form of problem solving. An agreement to refer a matter to an international court, by way of an ad hoc agreement on jurisdiction (*compromis*) or through a jurisdictional provision found in an international treaty delegating to it *ex ante* adjudicative power (such as a compromissory clause found in a specific treaty or a treaty provision entailing the general acceptance of 'compulsory' jurisdiction over disputes arising in a certain bilateral or multilateral context),[7] merely implies a choice by the relevant international actors to add adjudication to the tool box available to them for handling the policy problem at hand. Other political or diplomatic measures are still likely to be utilized before, after and in tandem with the adjudicative process.

For example, parallel to the establishment of the International Criminal Tribunal for Yugoslavia (ICTY) by Resolutions 808 (1993) and 827 (1993),[8] the Security Council has taken other measures designed to facilitate the resolution, or at least the management, of the conflict in the Balkans, including sanctions against the Former Yugoslavia, the dispatch of peacekeepers to the region (UNPROFOR) and several political initiatives.[9] Hence, the establishment of the ICTY

6 *Northern Cameroons* (*Cameroon* v. *UK*), 1963 ICJ 15, 34.

7 See e.g. Convention on the Prevention and Punishment of the Crime of Genocide, 9 December 1948, in force 12 January 1951, art. 9, 78 UNTS 277 (hereinafter 'Genocide Convention'); European Convention for the Peaceful Settlement of Disputes, Strasbourg, 29 April 1957, in force 30 April 1958, art. 1, ETS 23.

8 Security Council Resolution 808 (22 February 1993), preamble, UN Doc. S/RES/808 (1993); Security Council Resolution 827 (25 May 1993), preamble, UN Doc. S/RES/827 (1993).

9 See e.g. Security Council Resolution 787 (16 November 1992), UN Doc. S/RES/787 (1992).

served as one policy instrument alongside other policy tools designed to deal with the conflict and restore law and order to the region. In fact, in such a multiple-response environment, one possible objective for establishing the jurisdiction of an international tribunal is to create legal and political conditions that support the application of the other policy tools employed.[10]

Indeed, once international court jurisdiction is established, the shadow of adjudication may affect the manner in which other polices are likely to be implemented, even if the eventual solution for the problem at hand is to be reached through non-judicial avenues.[11] If the parties to a dispute can invoke at any point in time the jurisdiction of an international court applying international law norms, these norms are likely to serve as the benchmark against which the outcomes of any political process taking place in relation to the same dispute will be assessed. For example, it may be argued that the most dramatic impact of the 'compulsory' dispute-settlement procedures introduced under the post-1995 World Trade Organization (WTO) is to be found not in the few hundreds of cases that were actually litigated before the dispute-settlement panels, arbitrators and Appellate Body, but rather in the manner in which the *ex ante* conferral of jurisdiction to the WTO judicial or arbitral bodies has influenced the far larger group of cases resolved under the auspices of the WTO system without resort to adjudication (e.g. through consultation). Furthermore, the existence of compulsory jurisdiction may have also affected situations involving 'dogs that didn't bark' – that is, instances in which states decided not to violate WTO law in the first place because of the shadow of international adjudication.[12]

Similarly, the highest hopes many observers hold for the success of the International Criminal Court (ICC) do not necessarily boil down to expectations that the creation of the Court will lead to a sharp rise in the number of national or international trials for violations of international criminal law. Rather they hang on the possibility that the mere existence of the ICC jurisdiction may deter leaders and

[10] Shany, 'Assessing the Effectiveness of International Courts', pp. 43–44.

[11] For a classic exposition of the 'shadow of litigation' phenomenon, see Robert Mnookin and Lewis Kornhauser, 'Bargaining in the Shadow of the Law: The Case of Divorce' (1979) 79 *Yale Law Journal* 950.

[12] See e.g. Marc L. Busch and Eric Reinhardt, 'Bargaining in the Shadow of the Law: Early Settlement in GATT/WTO Disputes' (2000) 24 *Fordham International Law Journal* 158.

senior military personnel from committing international crimes to begin with. In the somewhat provocative words of the first ICC Prosecutor, Luis Moreno-Ocampo, delivered at his swearing-in ceremony: 'The effectiveness of the International Criminal Court should not be measured by the number of cases that reach it. On the contrary, complementarity implies that the absence of trials before this Court, as a consequence of the regular functioning of national institutions, would be a major success.'[13]

The combined effect of the empowerment of international courts by jurisdictional provisions and the shadow effect these provisions generate renders the study of jurisdiction a key aspect of the study of the legal power of international courts. Studying jurisdiction offers us an important prism through which we can examine the reach of international adjudication and its impact on the conduct of relevant international actors. Put differently, it allows us to appreciate the effects on international law and international relations of the case-selection choices made by the mandate providers, the parties to any specific dispute and international courts themselves.

Rules on admissibility, which allow international courts, under certain circumstances, to decline to adjudicate cases validly referred to them, represent another important object of study. The reason for this is that such rules afford international courts the power to introduce another layer of case selection, which may be, at times, more nuanced and context dependent than the *ex ante* case selection often exercised by the mandate providers and the parties to the dispute. Put differently, rules on admissibility provide international courts with policy tools that may help them to mitigate the impact of jurisdictional provisions and to defend their own institutional interests as well as the interests of some of their constituencies.

For example, the ICC Prosecutor may use the 'interests of justice' test provided in article 53 of the Rome Statute to refuse to initiate an investigation which could conflict with some of the broad policy goals underlying the ICC.[14] This allows the Prosecutor and the Court, which exercises supervision over this aspect of prosecutorial

[13] Statement made by Mr. Luis Moreno-Ocampo, June 16, 2003, www.icc-cpi.int/NR/rdonlyres/D7572226-264A-4B6B-85E3-2673648B4896/143585/030616_moreno_ocampo_english.pdf.

[14] See ICC Office of the Prosecutor, Policy Paper on the Interests of Justice (2007).

discretion,[15] to fine-tune the broad policies set by the mandate providers when establishing the Court, and to adapt them to specific conditions of the country situations where criminal investigation is being considered.

The advantages of resorting to adjudication

The choice of international courts as actual or potential dispute-settlement venues implies a policy choice to opt for a process providing legal norms a key role in influencing the outcome of disputes. With some rare exceptions (such as the power of some courts to decide cases *ex aequo et bono*),[16] international courts offer a law-based method for dispute settlement, involving the ascertainment of relevant sets of facts and the application of legal norms to the facts that were established. As suggested earlier, the shadow of international adjudication may strengthen the role of international legal norms in international life (and, consequently, contribute to a more robust international rule of law) even in situations that are not ultimately referred to adjudication.

The selection of international courts as dispute-settlement forums and the decision to judicialize a certain field of international relations (by bestowing international courts with 'compulsory' jurisdiction) are, however, not self-evident. Rather, they are policy choices. In this section, I will discuss some of the possible reasons that explain such policy choices and allow us to understand why international actors choose international courts rather than other, less law-based third party decision-making procedures, such as mediation or conciliation, for handling international disputes; and also to understand why, if a law-based approach is preferred, they may choose to entrust jurisdiction to permanent international courts, as opposed to other law-applying agents, such as international arbitration tribunals or national courts.

One possible motivation for the conferral of jurisdiction to international courts is the attraction many decision makers find in channelling dispute resolution to ostensibly objective law-based avenues.

[15] Rome Statute of the International Criminal Court, 17 July 1998, in force 1 July 2002, art. 53, 2187 UNTS 3 (hereinafter 'ICC Statute').

[16] See e.g. Statute of the International Court of Justice, annexed to the UN Charter, San Francisco, 26 June 1945, in force 24 October 1945, art. 38(2) (hereinafter 'ICJ Statute'); DSU, art. 26.

Compared to the vagaries of world politics, law-based dispute resolution offers the parties to a transaction (and interested third parties who may be influenced by the transaction) a relatively high degree of stability and predictability.[17] Law-based dispute resolution also conveys to the disputing parties and outside observers notions of fairness and equal treatment,[18] and projects a high degree of apolitical professionalism.[19] In addition, in many areas of international relations, law-based dispute resolution (by international courts or other actors operating under the shadow of adjudication) offers all stakeholders some guarantee that the outcome of the process will reflect the values and interests promoted by the relevant body of law (and by the legal regime to which this body of law belongs).[20] Lastly, some parties to international disputes may regard a law-based dispute settlement through establishing or invoking the jurisdiction of international adjudicative bodies as a particularly useful method for compartmentalizing certain aspects of their relationship affected by their dispute under specific legal categories and procedures, thereby preventing their disputes from spilling over into other aspects of their relationship.

To illustrate, a state and a foreign investor may agree in advance to resolve future disputes concerning an investment through a law-based dispute-settlement mechanism such as arbitration. This

[17] See e.g. DSU, art. 3(2) ('The dispute settlement system of the WTO is a central element in providing security and predictability to the multilateral trading system'). See also DSU, art 17(5) and Appendix III. But see Jose E. Alvarez, 'The New Dispute Settlers: (Half) Truths and Consequences' (2003) 38 *Texas International Law Journal* 405, 440.

[18] See e.g. Laurence Boisson de Chazournes and Philippe Sands, 'Introduction', in Laurence Boisson de Chazournes and Philippe Sands (eds.), *International Law, the International Court of Justice and Nuclear Weapons* (Cambridge: Cambridge University Press, 1999), p. 19 ('Courts generally provide a more level playing field than political fora').

[19] See e.g. Moshe Cohen-Eliya and Iddo Porat, 'Proportionality and the Culture of Justification' (2011) 59 *American Journal of Comparative Law* 463, 483; Timothy William Waters, 'A Kind of Judgment: Searching for Judicial Narratives after Death' (2010) 42 *George Washington International Law Review* 279, 287.

[20] E.g., even when the European Court of Human Rights (ECtHR) lends its services to the achievement of a 'friendly settlement', any agreement reached must be consistent with a law-based outcome. Convention on the Protection of Human Rights and Fundamental Freedoms, 4 November 1950, in force 3 September 1953, art. 39(1), ETS 5 (hereinafter 'ECHR') ('At any stage of the proceedings, the Court may place itself at the disposal of the parties concerned with a view to securing a friendly settlement of the matter on the basis of respect for human rights as defined in the Convention and the Protocols thereto').

increases the stability and predictability of the underlying transaction (the foreign investment) and offers the investor guarantees of fair treatment by an objective professional body in connection with any future grievances. To the extent that the applicable law before such a dispute-settlement mechanism is international investment law, the investor is also guaranteed that the process would be infused by a body of law, designed to protect foreign investors against unfair and inequitable treatment and the like. Finally, in the event of a dispute between the investor and the state, the parties will be able with relative ease to refer the transaction giving rise to the dispute to adjudication – thereby 'boxing it out' from other transactions they are engaged in – and to maintain business as usual with regard to their other dealings.

For all these reasons, some international actors, constituencies and observers may perceive law-based dispute resolution as more legitimate and effective than diplomatic or other power-based third party dispute resolution alternatives, such as mediation or conciliation.[21] In fact, several commentators have claimed that the de-politicization of some international conflicts and certain areas of international relations through the conferral of jurisdiction on international courts is one of the greatest achievements of contemporary international law (especially in the field of international economic law).[22]

There are also specific reasons why mandate providers and disputing parties select *international courts* as their preferred dispute-settlement venue for addressing certain policy problems or as preferred permanent venues for adjudicating recurring disputes, as opposed to other law-applying mechanisms such as international arbitration tribunals or domestic courts. Most significantly, permanent international courts enjoy particularly high levels of social legitimacy in the eyes of relevant audiences because of their institutional independence and impartiality, which are generally viewed

[21] See Erik Voeten, 'Public Opinion and the Legitimacy of International Courts' (2013) 14 *Theoretical Inquiries in Law* 411, 423–424.

[22] See e.g. Ibrahim F. I. Shihata, *Towards a Greater Depoliticization of Investment Disputes: The Roles of ICSID and MIGA* (ICSID Publication, 1992); Christina L Davis, *Why Adjudicate? Enforcing Trade Rules in the WTO* (Princeton, NJ: Princeton University Press, 2012), p. 93 (describing the tendency for 'fighting with friends' as a side effect of depoliticized dispute settlements); Luke Peterson, 'Out of Order', in Michael Waibel *et al.* (eds.), *The Backlash against Investment Arbitration: Perception and Reality* (Alphen aan den Rijn: Kluwer Law International, 2010), p. 501.

by relevant constituencies as important building blocks of a fair and legitimate process.[23] In addition, the permanence enjoyed by international courts ensures a degree of functional stability and predictability of outcome that, in turn, enables them to build over time a reputation of fairness and professionalism, thereby enhancing the perceived objectivity of their operations.[24] Naturally, there may be cases where stability of process and predictability of outcome is a drawback of international courts – for instance, where the procedure is excessively cumbersome, and the outcome inconsistent with the values and interests held by potential litigants. Furthermore, a reputation for fairness and professionalism can be lost over time, not only enhanced. Thus, it is by a process akin to 'natural selection' that some international courts have established themselves over time as the preferred forums for dispute settlement in certain fields of law, with respect to some potential parties, while others have failed to gain similar support and to attract significant levels of actual or potential business.[25]

Some international actors may prefer to grant jurisdiction over international disputes to international courts rather than national courts. Whereas national courts may find it difficult to maintain their neutrality in international disputes involving their own state, international courts are typically not being perceived as having a priori disposition for or against any of the parties involved in an international dispute. As a result, conferring jurisdiction on international courts may seem more consistent with the expectation that international adjudication be conducted according to the equality of arms principle.[26] Furthermore, to the extent that international law

[23] See e.g. Lakshman Guruswamy, 'Commentary on "Equipping the ICJ to Deal with Developing Areas of International Law: Environmental Law"', in Connie Peck and Roy S Lee (eds.), *Increasing the Effectiveness of the International Court of Justice: Proceedings of the ICJ/UNITAR Colloquium to Celebrate the 50th Anniversary of the Court* (The Hague: Kluwer Law International, 1997), pp. 428–429.

[24] Naturally, however, in some contexts, the flexibility associated with adjudication before international arbitration tribunals constitutes a considerable advantage that outweighs the benefits of adjudication before an international court. See e.g. J.G. Merrills, *International Dispute Settlement*, 5th edn (Cambridge: Cambridge University Press, 2011), p. 111.

[25] See e.g. Shabtai Rosenne and Yaël Ronen, *The Law and Practice of the International Court of Justice 1920–2005*, 4 vols. (Leiden: Martinus Nijhoff Publishers, 2006), vol. I, p. 13.

[26] See e.g. Mohamed Shahabuddeen, 'The World Court at the Turn of the Century', in A.S. Muller, D. Raic and J.M. Thuranszky (eds.), *The International Court of Justice: Its Future Role After Fifty Years* (The Hague: Martinus Nijhoff Publishers, 1997),

mirrors more closely than national law notions of international justice and reflects more widely accepted political preferences and societal values, authorizing international courts to settle disputes through the application of international law may be regarded by some potential litigants as more desirable, morally and socially, than settling the same disputes before national courts. The reason for this is that many national courts are limited by their own national law in the degree to which they can apply international law and have more limited expertise in doing so.[27] Here, too, a process of 'natural selection' may lead parties to some international interactions to prefer international courts. In other instances, parties may prefer national courts (which also offer certain advantages, such as their generally superior enforcement powers).[28]

Using Thomas Franck's vocabulary of international legitimacy – centred around notions of *determinacy, symbolic validation, coherence* and *adherence* as legitimating factors – one may identify in the structures, procedures and outcomes of international courts all four of Franck's legitimacy-enhancing features.[29] These features may help explain the choice made by mandate providers to establish permanent international courts, as well as the decision by specific disputing parties to invoke their jurisdiction.

First, through their accumulative jurisprudence, international courts help to elucidate and concretize the norms of international law governing specific fields of international relations, thereby imbuing them with a relatively high degree of determinacy. International courts thus increase the legitimacy of any demand made from parties appearing before them that is based on a relevant legal norm and create forward-looking precedents (albeit of a nominally non-binding nature for third parties),[30] which may further increase the determinacy of the norms in question and enhance the legitimacy of future law application efforts.

pp. 3, 20; Mark L. Movsesian, 'Sovereignty, Compliance, and the World Trade Organization: Lessons from the History of Supreme Court Review' (1999) 20 *Michigan Journal of International Law* 775, 792.

27 See e.g. Andre Nolkaemper, *National Courts and the International Rule of Law* (Oxford: Oxford University Press, 2011), p. 6.

28 See e.g. Eric A Posner, *The Perils of Global Legalism* (Chicago: The University of Chicago Press, 2009), p. 174.

29 Thomas M Franck, *The Power of Legitimacy among Nations* (New York, Oxford: Oxford University Press, 1990), p. 47.

30 See e.g. ICJ Statute, art. 59.

Second, the choice to entrust international courts with jurisdiction over disputes draws upon the reputation of other courts, national and international, as symbols of procedural fairness and substantive justice. The legitimizing effect accruing from the external similarity of many features in international courts to their domestic counterparts (from the physical layout of the courtroom[31] to the appellation 'judges' used to describe international adjudicators) may be further strengthened by the symbolic validation associated with using positive value-laden terms in their official titles. This may explain why the principal judicial organ of the United Nations is called the International Court of *Justice* and the Strasbourg Court is named the European Court of *Human Rights*.

Third, while not subject to a formal system of binding precedents, international courts tend to opt for consistent law interpretation and uniform law application.[32] Their commitment to Franck's principle of coherence not only increases legal certainty, as noted before, but also corresponds to the principle of justice that similar cases should be treated alike. This further enhances the legitimacy of court adjudication.

Finally, by respecting the boundaries of their jurisdictional configuration, international courts adhere in their work to the principle of legality, and in particular to the specific second-order principles of jurisdiction that govern their power to pronounce upon the law. Thus, law-based dispute settlement before a court governed by law draws its legitimacy from the same source of its overarching legal order.

Consequently, it is not surprising that the removal of judicial decision making from the unwieldy realm of political struggles to the realm of principled law-based decision making by international courts legitimizes international dispute settlement (or, more broadly, international problem solving) in the eyes of important constituencies.[33] Again, this does not mean that the establishment

[31] See Judith Resnick and Dennis Curtis, *Representing Justice: Invention, Controversy and Rights in City-States and Democratic Court Rooms* (New Haven: Yale University Press, 2011), p. 225 *et seq.*

[32] See e.g. Raj Bhala, 'The Precedent Setters: De Facto Stare Decisis in WTO Adjudication' (1999) 9 *Florida State University Journal of Transnational Law and Policy* 1; Mohammed Shahabuddeen, *Precedent in the World Court* (Cambridge: Cambridge University Press, 2007), p. 107.

[33] *Cf.* Philip Allot, 'The International Court and the Voice of Justice', in Vaughan Lowe and Malgosia Fitzmaurice (eds.), *Fifty Years of the International Court of Justice*

of the jurisdiction of international courts renders all other alternatives redundant or even less legitimate after international courts have entered into the picture. Indeed, the opposite may be true. For example, it seems plausible that the referral of the Libya situation to the ICC may have conferred considerable legitimacy on the sanctions regime imposed by the Security Council and perhaps even on NATO's subsequent military intervention in the civil war in that country.[34]

Nevertheless, conferring jurisdiction on an international court does not come free of cost in terms of available policy choices. The introduction of the possibility of international adjudication may constrain the policy options available to the relevant mandate providers and disputing parties in managing the relevant policy problem. First, the decision to resolve a political problem through law-based methods often entails a narrowing of the possible outcomes of the dispute-settlement process. Courts do not typically engage in package deals, nor are they necessarily inclined to adopt 'splitting the difference' type of solutions.[35] As already noted, the existence of a law-based dispute-settlement option casts a shadow over other dispute-settlement avenues. Consequently, once 'compulsory' jurisdiction providing for the enforcement of legal rights through judicial means has been established, the scope of politically acceptable solutions may be altered. This is because decision makers may be less inclined to concede interests, which are captured by judicially enforceable rights, than when the same interests are protected by legal rights that are non-enforceable in nature or are not legally protected at all. In the same vein, decision makers may be ready to change their substantive position under the looming thereat of adjudication. Indeed, it has been suggested, for example, that

(Cambridge: Cambridge University Press, 1996), p. 33 (claiming that only courts can legitimize the application of public legal power).

34 See e.g. Mark Kersten, 'The ICC in Libya: Beyond Peace and Justice', *OpenCanada.org: Canada's Blog for International Affairs*, 9 May 2012, http://opencanada.org/features/the-think-tank/comments/the-icc-in-libya-beyond-peace-vs-justice/. It is also possible that the lack of agreement in the Security Council to refer the civil war in Syria, which started in 2011, to the ICC has made it more difficult to justify humanitarian interventions in the conflict.

35 Richard B. Bilder, 'Some Limitations of Adjudication as an International Dispute Settlement Technique' (1982) 23 *Virginia Journal of International Law* 1, 3. However, see Yuval Shany, 'Bosnia, Serbia and the Politics of International Adjudication' (2008) 45 *Justice* 21 (criticizing the Court for striving too hard to reach a balanced outcome in its judgment).

WTO members are more likely to agree in bilateral consultations to the removal of controversial trade measures when a panel ruling is impending than when a dispute-settlement panel has not yet been convened, rendering the prospects of law enforcement less imminent.[36]

A second and related point is that international courts tend, once activated, to frame issues in ways that change the way in which the dispute or policy problem is understood.[37] This, in turn, also constrains the policy options available to political actors. For example, once the ICC issued arrest warrants in 2011 against Muammar Gaddafi and two senior aides for their suspected involvement in crimes against humanity, a settlement of the Libyan civil war in ways oblivious to the criminal responsibility of the heads of the Gaddafi regime became a much less plausible policy alternative for those parties involved in diplomatic efforts to resolve the situation in Libya.[38]

Finally, the actual submission of a dispute to an international court may affect the motivation of some of the disputing parties to engage in diplomatic negotiations potentially leading to a political settlement. Although in many cases initiating litigation increases pressure to settle,[39] in certain cases litigation can create the opposite effect, creating pressure not to settle. For example, it could be argued that the ICJ advisory opinions in the *Western Sahara*[40] case and in the *Wall in the Occupied Palestinian Territories* case[41] hardened the negotiating positions of the parties, favoured by the said opinions (Polisario and the Palestinian Liberation Organization) in

[36] Busch and Reinhardt, 'Early settlement in GATT/WTO disputes', 163.

[37] See e.g. Karen J. Alter, 'Agents or Trustees? International Courts in their Political Context', in Karen J Alter (ed.), *The European Courts' Political Powers: Selected Essays* (Oxford: Oxford University Press, 2009), p. 262 ('Rulings and interpretations by international judges may help shape international rhetorical politics').

[38] See e.g. Kevin Govern, 'Avoiding Amnesty: Bringing Gaddafi to Justice', JURIST – Forum, 25 August 2011, http://jurist.org/forum/2011/08/kevin-govern-gaddafi-icc.php.

[39] See e.g. Joseph A. Conti, *Between Law and Diplomacy: The Social Context of Disputing at the World Trade Organization* (Stanford, CA: Stanford University Press, 2010), p. 130.

[40] *Western Sahara*, 1975 ICJ 12.

[41] *Legal Consequences of the Construction of a Wall in the Occupied Palestinian Territories*, 2004 ICJ 136, 160 ('It is not clear, however, what influence the Court's opinion would have on [ongoing] negotiations: participants in the present proceedings have expressed differing views in this regard').

ways which made it more difficult for them to surrender their internationally recognized rights, notwithstanding their political and military weakness.[42] If this is true, then the issuance of these two opinions might have complicated the political processes designed to settle the two conflicts, contributing to their perception as intractable in nature.[43]

[42] See e.g. International Crisis Group Middle East, *Western Sahara: Out of the Impasse* (2007) 9. *Cf.* Dore Gold and Diane Morrison, *Discussion on Whether the Declaration Lodged by the Palestinian Authority Meets Statutory Requirements: Historical and Diplomatic Considerations* (NGO Roundtable, 19–20 October 2010, Office of the Prosecutor, International Criminal Court) 35.

[43] See e.g. Samuel J. Spector, 'Western Sahara and the Self-Determination Debate' (Summer 2009) 16 *Middle East Quarterly* 33 (The ICJ Advisory Opinion and Western Sahara and the immediate reactions thereto by Morocco, Spain and the General Assembly has set the stage for decades of stalemate in Western Sahara); Charles F. Martel, 'Give Peace a Chance: How Considering Peace Process Obligations Would Have Improved the Rulings of the International Court of Justice and the Israeli Supreme Court on the Israeli Security Barrier' (2007) 17 *Duke Journal of Comparative and International Law* 305 (criticizing the *Wall* Opinion's detachment from the legal agreements comprising the Israeli–Palestinian peace process).

2

Jurisdiction as delegated authority

Foundational and specific jurisdiction

Regardless of whether conferral of jurisdiction upon an international court creates new policy options for international actors or constrains existing ones, an important effect of jurisdiction conferral is the legal empowerment of international courts to adjudicate a case. As explained later in this section, entrusting courts with jurisdiction to adjudicate cases implies a transfer of legal power from states and other international actors to international courts. The origins and process of transfer in turn affect the legitimacy and effectiveness of international courts.

Establishing the jurisdiction of international courts involves two separate expressions of will or intent by international actors denoting two distinct power transfers. International Court of Justice (ICJ) judge Daxner has alluded to the two transfers in his dissent in *Corfu Channel*:

> The word 'jurisdiction' has two fundamental meanings in international law. This word is used: (1) to recognize the Court as an organ instituted for the purpose *jus dicere* and in order to acquire the ability to appear before it; (2) to determine the competence of the Court, i.e., to invest the Court with the right to solve concrete cases[1]

The first meaning of jurisdiction – referred to hereinafter as the foundational jurisdiction or foundational authority of international courts – is determined, as a rule, by a multilateral treaty, which

[1] *Corfu Channel* (*UK* v. *Albania*), 1948 ICJ 15, 39 (Daxner J., dissenting).

normally serves as the relevant court's constitutive instrument.[2] It establishes the court, delineates the outer limits of its jurisdictional powers (*ratione personae, ratione materiae, ratione temporis, ratione loci*) and introduces a variety of jurisdictional conditions that regulate the exercise of jurisdiction in concrete cases (such as exhaustion of local remedies and consent to adjudication by the respondent party). Significantly, foundational jurisdiction only confers upon international courts a *potential* (or *in abstracto*) power to adjudicate certain categories of cases. The *actual* (or *in concreto*) power of the court to adjudicate any given dispute depends on a specific act of referral, which falls within the prescribed jurisdictional limits and meets the relevant jurisdictional conditions.[3]

A critical decision which the mandate providers must adopt when formulating the court's constitutive instrument, and the jurisdictional limits and conditions contained therein, is whether to confer upon the new court 'compulsory' or 'non-compulsory' jurisdiction. That is, whether or not to introduce a jurisdictional condition requiring the consent of both parties to the dispute for each specific exercise of jurisdiction by the court. A halfway solution adopted by the drafters of the ICJ Statute[4] and some other constitutive instruments of international courts[5] has been to allow interested member states to waive upon ratification, or at a later point in time, the jurisdictional condition requiring their specific consent for adjudication. Such opt-in 'compulsory jurisdiction' schemes apply

[2] One notable group of international tribunal established by an instrument other than a multilateral treaty is *ad hoc* international criminal tribunals, established by way of Security Council Resolutions. See e.g. Security Council Resolution 827 (1993), UN Doc. S/RES/827 (25 May 1993); Security Council Resolution 955 (1994), UN Doc. S/RES/955 (8 November 1994).

[3] Fitzmaurice proposes to treat specific jurisdiction as a question of *competence* (as opposed to jurisdiction, which he offers to limit to *general jurisdiction*). Gerald Fitzmaurice, 'The Law and Procedure of the International Court of Justice, 1951–4: Questions of Jurisdiction, Competence and Procedure' (1958) 34 Brit. Y.B. Int'l L. 8–9.

[4] ICJ Statute, Art. 36(2).

[5] See e.g. American Convention on Human Rights, 22 November 1969, in force 18 July 1978, Art. 62, OAS TS 36 (hereinafter 'ACHR'); Art. 46 of the ECHR (original text; article 46 was repealed in 1998 following the entry into force of Protocol 11); Protocol on the Establishment of an African Court of Human and Peoples' Rights, 9 June 1998, in force 25 January 2004, Art. 34(6), www.achpr.org/instruments/court-establishment (facilitating *ex ante* consent to individual and NGO complaints); United Nations Convention on the Law of the Sea, 10 December 1982, in force 16 November 1994, Art. 287, 1833 UNTS 397 (hereinafter 'UNCLOS').

in international courts authorized to adjudicate interstate disputes on a reciprocal basis (i.e. only when both parties to adjudication have made 'optional clause' type declarations). However, in human rights courts, where states typically occupy the position of respondents to claims brought by individuals or human rights commissions, the waiver by member states of the consent condition tends to be unilateral in nature.

The second meaning of jurisdiction, alluded to by Judge Daxner, refers to the specific authorization of an international court to hear a given case (this meaning of jurisdiction will be referred to hereinafter as specific jurisdiction). The court's specific jurisdiction over a given dispute depends on expression of intent by one or more of the disputing parties to utilize the pre-existing jurisdictional framework through seizing the court in a manner compatible with the terms of its foundational jurisdiction. Where the court's constitutive instruments contain a jurisdictional condition providing for party consent, the seizing of the court would confer upon it specific jurisdiction only if this condition had been met[6] (e.g. through the joint submission of the case to the court or by way of implicit consent to adjudication derived from the respondent party's failure to contest jurisdiction – *forum prorogatum*[7]).

The two types of international court jurisdiction, foundational and specific jurisdiction, involve authorization to adjudicate by two partly overlapping sets of international actors – the mandate providers and disputing parties. These two authorizations are subject to a particular temporal sequencing order: the foundational authorization of the court by the mandate providers predates its specific authorization by the parties.[8] Moreover, a normative hierarchy exists between the two levels of authorization. Foundational jurisdiction regulates and

[6] See *Factory at Chorzów* (*Germany* v. *Poland*) (Claim for Indemnity) (jurisdiction), 1927 PCIJ (ser A) No 9, at 32 ('When considering whether it has jurisdiction or not, the Court's aim is always to ascertain whether an intention on the part of the Parties exists to confer jurisdiction upon it').

[7] See e.g. Shabtai Rosenne, 'The Forum Prorogatum in the International Court of Justice' (1953) 6 *Revue hellénique de droit international* 1.

[8] See the distinction offered by the ICJ in the *Genocide* (*Bosnia* v. *Serbia*) case (2007) between questions of access to the court (foundational jurisdiction) and questions of jurisdiction (specific jurisdiction). *Application of the Convention on the Prevention and Punishment of the Crime of Genocide* (*Bosnia and Herzegovina* v. *Serbia and Montenegro*), 2007 ICJ 43, 85 ('[access] may be regarded as an issue prior to that of jurisdiction *ratione personae*' (emphasis added)).

constrains the power of the disputing parties to bestow upon international courts specific jurisdiction, and the disputing parties cannot extend the power of the courts beyond the foundational powers conferred upon it by the mandate providers. This is primarily because adding on new demands on international courts' time and resources, beyond those authorized by their mandate providers, would be tantamount to establishing new obligations for those mandate providers not involved in the specific case without their consent (such as an obligation to fund new forms of litigation or to enforce judgments emanating from such litigation) in violation of basic international law principles.[9]

In the light of the distinction between foundational and specific jurisdiction, how are we to understand instances in which potential parties to adjudication undertake in advance to accept a court's 'compulsory jurisdiction'? Such undertakings may appertain to future disputes arising under a particular treaty (facilitated by a compromissory clause found in that treaty)[10] or to all future disputes arising in respect of certain parties (facilitated by a general jurisdictional instrument, such as the General Act of 1928,[11] or by 'optional clause'-type declarations)?[12] Should we regard these manifestations of *ex ante* consent to adjudication as unilateral amendments to the court's foundational jurisdiction, transforming it, at least with regard to certain interactions between certain potential parties, from a 'non-compulsory jurisdiction' court to a 'compulsory jurisdiction' court? And if so, how is such a change in the nature of jurisdiction consistent with the assertion made above that parties to adjudication cannot, when granting international courts specific jurisdiction, deviate from the foundational jurisdiction established by the mandate providers?

To my mind, there is no contradiction between the parties' capacity to grant *ex ante* consent to adjudication and the hierarchical relationship between foundational and specific jurisdiction. For the

[9] *Cf.* Vienna Convention on the Law of Treaties, Vienna, 23 May 1969, in force 27 January 1980, arts. 34–35, 1155 UNTS 331 (hereinafter 'VCLT'). For further discussion, see pp. 73–75 of this book.

[10] See e.g. Art. 9 of the Genocide Convention.

[11] General Act for the Pacific Settlement of International Disputes, Geneva, 26 September 1928, in force 16 August 1929, Art. 17, 93 LNTS 344; Revised General Act for the Pacific Settlement of International Disputes, New York, 28 April 1949, in force 20 September 1950, Art. 17, 71 UNTS 101.

[12] ICJ Statute, Art. 36(2).

reasons explained later in this section, instruments authorizing a 'non-compulsory jurisdiction' court to exercise compulsory jurisdiction over future disputes (i.e. to exercise jurisdiction without obtaining any additional act of party consent) do not negate the foundational nature of the jurisdictional condition of consent; rather, they constitute a method by which the said condition is being fulfilled.

One possible understanding of legal instruments, such as compromissory clauses, providing *ex ante* consent to adjudication, is that they do not entail actual consent, but rather embody a commitment to grant consent in the future. Accordingly, they do not affect the jurisdictional structure of the court, but rather the future conduct of the parties to adjudication in relation to the court. Another approach, less strained perhaps, would regard some foundational jurisdictional conditions, including the additional consent requirement, as subject to a waiver. The voluntary nature of the consent requirement sits well with the view that the constitutive instrument of the 'non-compulsory jurisdiction' court's constitutive instrument only conferred upon the member states a waivable right to *refuse* consent to adjudication.[13] By adopting instruments providing for *ex ante* consent to adjudication, member states have exercised their right to fully or partially waive their right to refuse consent. If we accept that such a waiver is implicit in the foundational jurisdiction condition of additional consent, it is compatible with the aforementioned understanding of foundational jurisdiction as hierarchically superior to specific jurisdiction.

Jurisdiction as delegation

The precise legal import of establishing the foundational and specific jurisdiction of international courts may be better understood by reference to two related concepts, delegation and consent, which appear to be central in establishing the legality and legitimacy of international adjudication. Delegation is a key concept in understanding the powers of all international organizations. Unlike states, which in accordance with the *Lotus* principle enjoy all the powers that

[13] *Cf.* Hazel Fox and Philippa Webb, *The Law of State Immunity*, 3rd edn. (Oxford: Oxford University Press, 2013), p. 373 (discussing the ability of states to waive sovereign immunity after a dispute has arisen).

they have not surrendered *inter partes* or *erga omnes* through their international law obligations,[14] IGOs only enjoy those powers explicitly and implicitly attributed to them by states (some of the latter are sometimes understood as 'inherent powers').[15] Even when acting together, states cannot pass on to IGOs more powers than they cumulatively have. In the same way, IGOs cannot delegate to subsidiary bodies more powers than they themselves have received from their member states.[16]

The jurisdiction of international courts can be understood as a particular form of the delegation of power. It should be noted, however, that the exact nature of the power that has been delegated must be carefully defined. As explained in the ensuing pages, the jurisdiction of some international courts which serve as functional equivalents of national courts (such as international criminal tribunals or international investment tribunals) can be regarded as emanating from a delegation by states of power to adjudicate certain individuals or certain types of claims.[17] However, interstate courts such as the ICJ cannot receive adjudicative power over states through delegation from other states. Since states do not sit in judgment over one another (by virtue of the *par in parem non habet imperium* principle),[18] they cannot, strictly speaking, delegate to an international court the power to sit in judgment over the parties to interstate disputes. In the same vein, IGOs such as the Security Council, which have not been entrusted with judicial power over

[14] *SS 'Lotus' (France* v. *Turkey*), 1927 PCIJ (ser A) No. 10, at 18 ('International law governs relations between independent States. The rules of law binding upon States therefore emanate from their own free will as expressed in conventions or by usages generally accepted as expressing principles of law and established in order to regulate the relations between these co-existing independent communities or with a view to the achievement of common aims. Restrictions upon the independence of States cannot therefore be presumed').

[15] See Jan Klabbers, *An Introduction to International Institutional Law,* 2nd edn. (Cambridge: Cambridge University Press, 2009), p. 56.

[16] *Cf.* John Locke, *Second Treatise of Government,* new edn. (Nicholson Press, 2013) (originally published in 1690), p. 65 ('for nobody can transfer to another more power than he has in himself').

[17] See e.g. Yuval Shany, 'In Defense of Functional Interpretation of Article 12(3) of the Rome Statute – A Response to Yaël Ronen' (2010) 8 JICJ 329, 331–333 (arguing that the ICC Statute is partly based on delegation of criminal jurisdiction from states).

[18] Fox and Webb, *The Law of State Immunity,* pp. 26–27.

states or individuals, do not appear at first glance to have the capacity to transfer such powers onwards to an international court.[19]

Consequently, I would suggest that what states actually delegate to international courts when establishing their jurisdiction is not judicial power *per se*, but rather a decision-making power: The power to undertake legally binding decisions in connection with the interpretation and application of the delegating states' international obligations. According to this approach, adjudication serves as a modern-day substitute for the power of auto-interpretation or auto-determination enjoyed by states under the traditional concept of state sovereignty in classic international law.[20] Put differently, the process of determining the precise contents of legal obligations and their concrete application to a given set of circumstances, which states undertake on their own or negotiate with other states or international actors, can also be delegated to a third body – an international court – that will make the said determination through a process of adjudication.

Delegation may be conditional or unconditional in nature. For instance, the delegation of jurisdictional power to an international court can be made revocable, in accordance with the conditions found in the constitutive instrument establishing any particular international court.[21] Furthermore, the act of delegation may impose certain conditions on the empowered international court relating to the manner in which the delegated authority ought to be exercised. The most significant of the conditions appertaining to the decision-making power delegated to international courts is that their decisions must be reached through a judicial methodology: An independent and impartial judicial process of sorting out legal claims of the respective parties and establishing the relevant facts to which the legal findings would apply.

Because of the methodological limits that were imposed on them, the decision-making powers of international courts are considerably

19 This argument was raised by the defence in *Tadic* and rejected by the Appeals Chamber in its landmark 1995 decision on jurisdiction. *Prosecutor* v. *Tadic*, Decision on the Defense Motion for Interlocutory Appeal on Jurisdiction, 2 October 1995, [37]–[38].

20 See Leo Gross, 'States as Organs of International Law and the Problem of Autointerpretation', in Leo Gross, (ed.), *Essays on International Law and Organization* (New York: Transnational Publishers, Inc., 1984), p. 386.

21 See e.g. ACHR, Art. 78; ICC Statute, Art. 127.

narrower than those of the states which conferred jurisdiction upon them. For example, whereas disputing states may settle a case on the basis of *intra legem, praeter legem* and even *contra legem* considerations (at least in those cases where the applicable law is dispositive), international courts may, as a rule, only dispose of cases on the basis of *intra* or *infra legem* considerations.[22] Moreover, international courts must reach their conclusions within the restrictions found in their rules governing the admissibility of evidence and other aspects of fact-finding, whereas states may exercise their law application powers relying on a more flexible factual basis and fact-finding methods.

Delegation by IGOs

Specific questions about the permissibility of delegation to adjudicate and the nature of such delegation arise when political IGOs, not authorized themselves to exercise judicial powers, have invested international courts with jurisdiction. Such questions have on occasion been themselves the subject of adjudication. For instance, the 1954 ICJ Advisory Opinion on the *Effect of Awards of Compensation Made by the United Nations Administrative Tribunal (UNAT)* dealt with the question of whether the General Assembly had legal power to create a judicial tribunal that could generate judgments that would legally bind the United Nations Organization. The ICJ held that the United Nations Charter conferred upon the General Assembly the constitutional power to regulate the activities of the organization's Secretariat, and that such a power of regulation entailed an implicit authorization to establish a tribunal to settle disputes arising between the Secretariat and its staff:

[22] See e.g. *Frontier Dispute* (Burkina Faso/Mali), 1986 ICJ 554, 567 ('Since the Parties have not entrusted it with the task of carrying out an adjustment of their respective interests, it must also dismiss any possibility of resorting to equity *contra legem.* Nor will the Chamber apply equity *praeter legem.* On the other hand, it will have regard to equity *infra legem*'); *Free Zones of Upper Savoy and the District of Gex* (*France* v. *Switzerland*), 1932 PCIJ (Ser A/B) No. 46, at 153 ('While it is certain that the Parties, being free to dispose of their rights, might have embodied, in the negotiations contemplated in Article 1, paragraph 2, of the Special Agreement, and might also in any future negotiations embody in their agreement any provisions they might desire, and, accordingly, even abolish the free zones or settle matters lying outside the framework of the régime with which Article 2 of the Special Agreement deals, it in no way follows that the Court enjoys the same freedom').

In these circumstances, the Court finds that the power to establish a tribunal, to do justice as between the Organization and the staff members, was essential to ensure the efficient working of the Secretariat, and to give effect to the paramount consideration of securing the highest standards of efficiency, competence and integrity. Capacity to do this arises by necessary intendment out of the Charter.[23]

The power to 'ensure the efficient working of the Secretariat' – that is, to regulate its operations – which was delegated to the General Assembly by the state parties to the United Nations Charter, thus implied the power to delegate authority to an international court to settle disputes over the rights and obligations created by the said regulation. Here, too, it is the decision-making power attendant to the power to regulate, and not the power to adjudicate, which lies at the basis of the delegation of power to a judicial body.[24]

In *Tadic*, the International Criminal Tribunal for Yugoslavia (ICTY) faced a challenge to the very lawfulness of its existence, based on the claim that the Security Council, lacking judicial power, could not create a judicial body. Like the ICJ in 1954, the Tribunal held in 1995 that the power to create a criminal court was implicitly granted to the Council alongside the explicit legal powers it obtained under the Charter to regulate situations compromising international peace and security:

The Security Council has resorted to the establishment of a judicial organ in the form of an international criminal tribunal as an instrument for the exercise of its own principal function of maintenance of peace and security, i.e. as a measure contributing to the restoration and maintenance of peace in the former Yugoslavia

In this case, the structure of delegated authority proceeds in the following manner: The United Nations member states had delegated to the Security Council decision-making powers to be applied in situations involving a threat to international peace and security, including, implicitly, the power to determine how to respond to

[23] *Effect of Awards of Compensation Made by the United Nations Administrative Tribunal*, 1954 ICJ 47, 57.

[24] IGOs may also have implicit power to create quasi-judicial bodies for monitoring their activities and ensuring the legality and propriety of their decisions. See e.g. International Bank for Reconstruction and Development, Resolution No. IBRD 93–10: 'The World Bank Inspection Panel', 22 September 1993, 34 ILM (1995) 520.

acts constituting international crimes. In turn, the Council delegated parts of this power to a subsidiary body – the ICTY – that was set up as a judicial body, that is to say an independent decision-making body operating based on a judicial methodology. The fact that the Council itself did not have judicial powers did not prevent it from delegating decision-making powers to a judicial body, which needs to apply them subject to a specific judicial methodology.[25]

Note, however, that the jurisdictional challenge in both *UNAT* and *Tadic* was ultimately levelled against the relevant IGOs for allegedly exceeding their own competence in creating judicial bodies. Such challenges do not typically arise with respect to international courts established directly by states (such as the ICJ or the European Court of Human Rights), as there is little doubt that states are entitled under international law to delegate legally binding decision-making authority to a third party. There is also little question that states may instruct the said third party to reach its decisions pursuant to a judicial methodology. Such a delegation of authority does not conflict with the notion of state sovereignty, but it has rather been regarded, since as early as the beginning of the twentieth century, as an 'enlightened' exercise of sovereignty.[26]

Shared decision making by IGOs and international courts

A particular form of delegation may be found when states delegate certain powers to IGOs and simultaneously authorize an international court (or committee) to exercise power of review over the manner in which the relevant IGO applies its delegated powers. Under such a configuration of delegation of power, the decision-making power delegated from the states is shared by the IGO and the

[25] See Erika De Wet, 'The Security Council as a Law Maker: The Adoption of (Quasi)-Judicial Decisions', in Rüdiger Wolfrum and Volker Röben, (eds.), *Developments of International Law in Treaty Making* (Berlin: Springer, 2005), p. 200.

[26] Baron Descamps, 'Report to the Conference from the Third Commission on Pacific Settlement of International Disputes', in James Brown Scott (ed.), *The Reports to the Hague Conferences of 1899 and 1907* (1917), p. 55 ('[I]t agrees with the just demands of sovereignty, of which it is only an enlightened exercise. For, if there is no power superior to the States which can force a judge upon them, there is nothing to oppose their selection of an arbitrator by common agreement to settle their disputes').

international court reviewing its activities: the latter operating as a check on the exercise of power of the former.

Some of the powers of review held by the International Tribunal for the Law of the Sea (ITLOS) Sea-Bed Disputes Chamber over the operations of the International Sea-Bed Authority and the powers of the Court of Justice of the European Union (CJEU) can be explained in such terms.[27] Since the ITLOS Chamber is *inter alia* authorized to review the legality of acts or omissions of the Authority and allegations relating to acts of the Authority which constitute excess of jurisdiction or misuse of power,[28] it serves as a check on the power delegated to the Authority to 'organize and control activities in the [Sea-Bed and Ocean floor] Area'.[29] In the same vein, the CJEU checks the power of the European Union organs for 'lack of competence, infringement of an essential procedural requirement, infringement of the Treaties or of any rule of law relating to its application or misuse of powers'.[30]

Delegation from domestic courts

Finally, states can also delegate to international courts powers typically possessed by their own national courts. In such cases, what has been delegated to the international courts is not a general decision-making power, but rather the power of states to adjudicate certain individual or specific claims. As a result of their power configuration as recipients of delegated power that normally resides with domestic judicial institutions, the relevant international courts operate as functional equivalents of national courts.

For example, it is possible to understand the power of the International Criminal Court (ICC) to exercise criminal jurisdiction instead of the territorial state or the state of nationality of the accused as a form of delegation of judicial power,[31] comparable to the ability

[27] UNCLOS, Art. 187 (covering *inter alia* disputes over acts and omissions of the International Seabed Authority, the contracts it has signed and the liability it may has incurred); Treaty on the Functioning of the European Union, 30 March 2010, Art. 263, OJ (C 83) 47 (2010) (hereinafter 'TFEU').

[28] UNCLOS, Art. 187(b). [29] UNCLOS, Art. 157. [30] TFEU, Art. 263(b).

[31] *Cf.* Judgment of the International Military Tribunal, 30 September–1 October 1946, 22 *The Trial of German Major War Criminals, Proceedings of the International Military Tribunal sitting at Nuremberg, Germany* 444 (in establishing the IMT, states 'have done together what any of them might have done singly; for it is not to be doubted that any nation has the right thus to set up special courts to administer law').

of states to delegate criminal jurisdiction to other states in certain contexts.[32] Similarly, the power of North American Free Trade Agreement (NAFTA) Chapter 19 panels to exercise jurisdiction over challenges to agency determinations of antidumping and countervailing duties instead of local administrative courts can be seen as reflective of a delegation of judicial power from national decision-makers to international arbitration;[33] and the potential power of ICSID tribunals to substitute the national courts of the host state in which the investment takes place can be seen as reflective of delegation of judicial power from national institutions to ICSID tribunals.[34]

Agents versus trustees

Viewing the grant of jurisdictional power to international courts as an act of delegation of decision-making power does not dispose of all of the important questions relating to the power relations between international courts and their national and international constituencies. Most significantly, understanding of conferral of jurisdiction as an act of delegation does not settle the long-standing debate as to whether international courts serve as agents or trustees of the state parties subject to their jurisdiction.[35]

[32] See e.g. European Convention on the Transfer of Proceedings in Criminal Matters, Strasbourg, 15 May 1972, in force 30 March 1978, E.T.S. 73; M Cherif Bassiouni, 'Introduction to Transfer of Criminal Proceedings', in *International Criminal Law: Multilateral and Bilateral Enforcement Mechanisms*, 3rd edn. (Leiden: Martinus Nijhoff Publishers, 2008), vol. II, p. 515.

[33] North American Free Trade Agreement, 17 December 1992, in force 1 January 1994, sec. 1904(1), ('As provided in this Article, each Party shall replace judicial review of final antidumping and countervailing duty determinations with binational panel review').

[34] Convention on the Settlement of Investment Disputes between States and Nationals of Other States, 18 March 1965, in force 14 October 1966, Art. 42(1), 575 UNTS 159 (hereinafter 'ICSID Convention') ('The Tribunal shall decide a dispute in accordance with such rules of law as may be agreed by the parties. In the absence of such agreement, the Tribunal shall apply the law of the Contracting State party to the dispute [including its rules on the conflict of laws] and such rules of international law as may be applicable').

[35] See e.g. Karen J Alter, 'Agents or Trustees? International Courts in Their Political Context' (2008) 14 EUR. J. INT'L REL. 33; Manfred Elsig and Mark A Polack, 'Agents, Trustees, and International Courts: The Politics of Judicial Appointment at the World Trade Organization' (2014) 20 EUR. J. INT'L REL. 391. See, more generally, Giandomenico Majone, 'Two Logics of Delegation: Agency and Fiduciary Relations in EU Governance' (2001) 2 *European Union*

This debate, which revolves around the degree of control the parties continue to exert over international courts following their establishment, hinges on different assessments of the nature of the discretionary powers that were delegated to any particular international court. Regarding courts as agents implies that they continue to be controlled by the wishes and expectation of the jurisdiction-conferring parties, whereas regarding courts as trustees implies that they may also exercise independent powers of discretion on behalf of third-party beneficiaries (e.g. the general public or political community), even if this is contrary to the immediate wishes and interests of the jurisdiction-conferring parties.[36] Both theories – agency and trusteeship – are consistent, however, with the understanding of jurisdiction as a delegation of decision-making power offered above. The two theories differ from each other only in their accounts of the scope of independent decision-making power that was actually delegated to international courts.

Jurisdiction as consent

While delegation delineates the scope of authority afforded to international courts by the mandate providers and the disputing parties, consent typically establishes the acceptance by the latter of the power of an international court to adjudicate a specific dispute. In this regard, consent operates not only as a legal condition of jurisdiction imposed by the mandate providers (like other conditions such as exhaustion of local remedies), but also as an important factor in legitimating the operation of international courts, ensuring, in Frankian terms, the *adherence* of international adjudication with one basic principle, if not the most basic principle of the international legal system (at least in the age of voluntarism): the principle of state consent as the basis of international law obligations.[37]

In the words of the Permanent Court of International Justice (PCIJ) in *Eastern Carelia* (1923):

> This rule [of consent], moreover, only accepts and applies a principle which is a fundamental principle of international-law, namely, the principle of the

Politics 103; Darren Hawkins *et al.* (eds.), *Delegation and Agency in International Organizations* (Cambridge, MA: Cambridge University Press, 2006).

36 Alter, 'Agents or Trustees?', 55.

37 See e.g. Lassa Oppenheim, *International Law – A Treatise: Peace*, 3rd edn. (edited by Ronald F Roxburgh, London: Longmans, Green & Co., 1920–1921) (Reprinted 2006 by The Lawbook Exchange, Ltd.), vol. I, pp. 15–19.

independence of States. It is well established in international law that no State can, without its consent, be compelled to submit its disputes with other States either to mediation or to arbitration, or to any other kind of pacific settlement.[38]

When state consent to adjudication is lacking, or is alleged to be lacking, the exercise of jurisdiction by a court may be susceptible to serious legality and legitimacy challenges. Indeed, one may cite numerous instances in which such challenges focused – rightly or wrongly – on lack of consent to adjudication involving certain actors or issues. Lack of consent, for instance, underscored the United States' attack against the legitimacy of the ICJ in the aftermath of the Court's controversial judgment in the jurisdictional phase of the *Nicaragua* case and was cited as a principal reason for the need to modify the United States' acceptance of the 'compulsory jurisdiction' of the ICJ.[39] Similarly, the United States' attempts to delegitimize the ICC[40] and Serb attempts to delegitimize the ICTY[41] have often focused on their lack of consent to the exercise of jurisdiction by an international criminal tribunal over their nationals. Finally, although the demise of the Southern African Development Community (SADC) Court can be attributed to a perception by some member states that it has exceeded the competence which the member states had agreed to delegate to it under the Court's constitutive treaty, Zimbabwe – the Court's harshest critic – has also alleged lack of consent to the Protocol establishing the Court by more than one-third of the membership of SADC (including Zimbabwe itself).[42]

[38] *Eastern Carelia*, 1923 PCIJ (ser. B) (No. 5), at 27.

[39] See e.g. Statement issued by the US Department of State on Withdrawal from Proceedings in the Nicaragua case, 18 January 1985. Less than a year later, the US terminated its acceptance of the Court's jurisdiction under the 'Optional Clause'. United States Department of State Letter and Statement concerning Termination of Acceptance of ICJ Compulsory Jurisdiction, 24 ILM (1985) 1742.

[40] See e.g. US Secretary of Defense Rumsfeld Statement on the ICC Treaty, 6 May 2002; US Under Secretary for Political Affairs – Department of State, Marc Grossman, American Foreign Policy and the International Criminal Court, 6 May 2002.

[41] See e.g. Laura A Dickinson, 'The Relationship between Hybrid Courts and International Courts: The Case of Kosovo' (2003) 37 New England L. Rev. 1059, 1066–1067.

[42] See e.g. Frederick Cowell, 'The Death of the Southern African Development Community Tribunal's Human Rights Jurisdiction' (2013) 13 Hum. Rts. L. Rev. 153, 164; Laurie Nathan, 'The Disbanding of the SADC Tribunal: A Cautionary Tale' (2013) 35 *Human Rights Quarterly* 870, 876.

In this context, one may recall Fitzmaurice's perceptive remark that all ICJ cases where jurisdictional challenges are raised reveal less than full consent to the jurisdiction of the Court.[43] Put in Frankian legitimacy terms, Fitzmaurice's insight may be tied to the problem of lack of determinacy afflicting certain jurisdictional provisions. International courts deriving their jurisdiction from indeterminate legal texts may be more vulnerable to legitimacy challenges than courts relying on clear jurisdictional bases. In such cases, lack of consent may reflect a perceived problem of legitimacy, and result in even a greater problem – lack of acceptance of the relevant court's authority to adjudicate the dispute in question.

Awareness of the need to avoid the serious legitimacy challenges stemming from the lack of genuine consent to adjudication appears to have led international courts, such as the ICJ, to adopt a high threshold for what constitutes a valid expression of consent in some of its jurisprudence. For example, in *Aegean Sea* the Court held that an instrument not reflecting immediate and unconditional consent could not serve as the basis of *ad hoc* jurisdiction;[44] and in *Mutual Assistance in Criminal Matters*, which discussed the conditions for extricating implicit consent from state conduct under the *forum prorogatum*, the Court held:

> The consent allowing for the Court to assume jurisdiction must be certain. That is so, no more and no less, for jurisdiction based on *forum prorogatum*. As the Court has recently explained, whatever the basis of consent, the attitude of the respondent State must 'be capable of being regarded as 'an unequivocal indication' of the desire of that State to accept the Court's jurisdiction in a 'voluntary and indisputable' manner.[45]

In the same vein, we might regard the refusal by the ICJ to construe reservations to optional clauses declarations in a restrictive manner (*contra proferentem*)[46] as an attempt by the Court to ensure that its jurisdiction remains firmly grounded in the principle of state consent.

[43] Gerald Fitzmaurice, 'The Law and Procedure of the International Court of Justice' (1950) 27 Brit. Y.B. Int'l L. 1, 10–11.

[44] *Aegean Sea Continental Shelf* (*Greece* v. *Turkey*), 1978 ICJ 3, 44. See also *Genocide Convention* (*Bosnia and Herzegovina* v. *Yugoslavia*), 1996 ICJ 595, 618 (preliminary objections).

[45] *Certain Questions of Mutual Assistance in Criminal Matters* (*Djibouti* v. *France*), 2008 ICJ 177, 204.

[46] *Fisheries Jurisdiction* (*Spain* v. *Canada*), 1998 ICJ 432, 453.

3

Jurisdiction as a power constraint on international courts

Power implications of jurisdictional conditions

Jurisdiction reflects the totality of legal powers allocated to international courts. It also defines the limits imposed on these powers. For example, personal jurisdiction limits the identity of the natural or legal persons who can be subject to the court's authority, while subject-matter jurisdiction limits the scope of issues which can be reviewed by the relevant judicial body. Moreover, numerous conditions attendant to the grant of jurisdiction, such as consent by the disputing parties, exhaustion of domestic remedies and the lack of an alternative judicial forum that the parties may seize, further constrain the legal power of international courts.

Such jurisdictional conditions may originate from one of the following three sources: (1) the constitutive instrument of the relevant international court – that is, from the same mandate providers that conferred upon the court foundational jurisdiction[1]; (2) the specific legal instrument representing the consent of the parties to the court's jurisdiction (if such consent is needed);[2] or (3) general international law. An example of the latter source of a jurisdictional condition can

[1] See e.g. ICJ Statute, Art. 36; ECHR, Art. S; ICC Statute, Arts. 12 and 17.

[2] See e.g. Declaration by the United Kingdom of Great Britain and Northern Ireland recognizing the jurisdiction of the Court as compulsory, 5 July 2004, www.icj-cij.org/jurisdiction/index.php?p1=5&p2=1&p3=3&code=GB (excluding from the Court's jurisdiction 'any dispute which the United Kingdom has agreed with the other Party or Parties thereto to settle by some other method of peaceful settlement'). See also *Armed Activities on the Territory of the Congo* (*DRC* v. *Rwanda*), 2006 ICJ 6, 39 ('The Court recalls in this regard that its jurisdiction is based on the consent of the parties and is confined to the extent accepted by them [cite omitted]. When that consent is expressed in a compromissory clause in an

be found in Elettronica Sicula S.p.A. (ELSI), where the International Court of Justice (ICJ) held that exhaustion of domestic remedies is a condition emanating from general international law and governs, unless stipulated upon by the parties, investment claims, over which they exercise diplomatic protection. Hence, the condition applies even though it was not included in the instrument which conferred jurisdiction upon the Court.[3]

As explained in Parts II and III of this book, the authority-constraining effect of conditions such as consent, exhaustion of local remedies or no-multiplicity of proceedings renders them matters of jurisdiction and not of admissibility. This distinction was embraced by the ICJ in *Armed Activities on the Territory of the Congo* (*Democratic Republic of the Congo (DRC)* v. *Rwanda*), where the Court held that conditions found in a relevant compromissory clause (article 29 of the Convention on the Elimination of All Forms of Discrimination against Women (CEDAW)), which require exhaustion of other international dispute settlement procedures prior to seizing the Court, must be regarded as limits on party consent to adjudication. According to the Court, the limit-on-consent feature renders such conditions a matter of jurisdiction rather than admissibility.[4] Still, as I discuss in the ensuing pages, a further distinction must be made between conditions that deprive the relevant international court of the power to adjudicate the dispute in question and conditions that afford courts discretion to decide whether or not to exercise their legal powers. I will classify the latter category of conditions as raising questions of admissibility and not of jurisdiction, although they have jurisdiction-constraining or limit-on-consent implications.

In any case, important restrictions apply to the ability of the disputing parties to agree upon new jurisdictional conditions that affect the jurisdictional structure or foundational powers of international courts. Such restrictions emanate primarily from the different hierarchical status of the conflicting instruments: The power to attach

international agreement, any conditions to which such consent is subject must be regarded as constituting the limits thereon').

[3] *Elettronica Sicula S.p.A. (ELSI)* (*USA* v. *Italy*), 1989 ICJ 15, 42 ('the Chamber finds itself unable to accept that an important principle of customary international law should be held to have been tacitly dispensed with, in the absence of any words making clear an intention to do so').

[4] *Armed Activities on the Territory of the Congo* (*DRC* v. *Rwanda*), 2006 ICJ 6, 39–40. The holding was cited with approval in *Mutual Assistance in Criminal Matters* (*Djibouti* v. *France*), 2008 ICJ 177, 201.

jurisdictional conditions to consent-granting statements may be limited explicitly or implicitly by the foundational instrument that establishes the Court and regulates the parties' ability to confer upon it specific jurisdiction.

Thus, for example, in the *Use of Force (NATO)*, the ICJ adopted a narrow construction of article 35(2) of the Statute, regulating access to the court by states not parties to the Statute (or, in my terminology, foundational personal jurisdiction) in a manner that excludes reliance on post-1945 specific jurisdictional agreements. It justified its restrictive stance on this question of interpretation in the following terms:

> The object and purpose of Article 35 of the Statute is to define the conditions of access to the Court ... [I]t would have been inconsistent with the main thrust of the text to make it possible in the future for States to obtain access to the Court simply by the conclusion between themselves of a special treaty, multilateral or bilateral, containing a provision to that effect.[5]

The specific legal construction offered by the Court that finds a conflict between article 35 and the relevant compromissory clause (article IX of the Genocide Convention) seems questionable. There is no obvious reason why the mandate providers would have wished to prevent the utilization of the Court by non-member states, given its broad dispute settlement function and international peace and security-promoting mission. Nevertheless, the principle expounded in the *Use of Force (NATO)*, according to which the foundational jurisdiction of the Court limits the space left for disputing parties to conclude specific jurisdictional agreements or introduce specific jurisdictional conditions that deviate from its scope of conferred authority, is no doubt correct.

Moreover, restricting the power of disputing parties to shape the foundational jurisdiction of international courts and to add new jurisdictional conditions may be defended not only by way of allusion to formal legal hierarchy, but also, at times, through considerations of international court legitimacy and effectiveness. Judge Lauterpacht's famous dissents in *Norwegian Loans* and *Interhandel* are two examples of the proposition that the terms of the ICJ's specific jurisdiction should be sometimes limited in order to maintain its legitimacy. When confronted with the Connally Amendment, which contained a self-judging clause, excluding from the purview of the United States' consent to the

[5] *Legality of the Use of Force* (*Serbia and Montenegro* v. *Belgium*), 2004 ICJ 279, 319.

ICJ's compulsory jurisdiction disputes that the United States itself designated as falling under its domestic jurisdiction.[6] Lauterpacht took the view that the terms of the clause conflicted with the principle that the Court must serve as the ultimate arbiter of its own jurisdiction, enshrined in article 36(6) of the Statute (the *compétence de la compétence* provision).[7] The authority to determine whether or not jurisdiction can be found, which Lauterpacht regarded as 'an indispensable element of legal obligation' and part of the constitutional make-up of the ICJ, could not be stipulated on by the parties.[8]

In his dissents, Lauterpacht appears to have been primarily concerned about the need to protect the perceived authority (i.e. legitimacy)[9] of the court to have the final word on the interpretation and application of its own Statute. Consequently, he was of the view that the Court should reject terms in a specific jurisdictional instrument that subject a core judicial function – the independent factual and legal determination of whether conditions for jurisdiction have been fulfilled – to external political control. Hence, Lauterpacht believed that the disputing parties could have decided whether or not to grant legal power to the Court pursuant to article 36(2) of the Statute, but they could not stipulate that their own exercise of decision-making power would override that of the Court after the latter had obtained legal authority over any aspect of the dispute (including, whether it is competent to adjudicate it).[10] Delegation of authority to exercise decision-making power must therefore be, in a sense, irreversible. Once the parties authorize the Court to decide the dispute, they lose their unilateral law interpretation and law application powers in connection with the legal disposition of the case. While the parties retain the power to remove a dispute from the docket by settling it out of court (a joint exercise of decision-making

[6] US declaration recognizing the Jurisdiction of the Court as Compulsory, 2 August 1946, 1 UNTS 9 ('such declaration shall not apply to ... disputes with regard to matters which are essentially within the domestic jurisdiction of the United States as determined by the United States').

[7] *Interhandel* (*Switzerland* v. *US*), 1959 ICJ 6, 101 (Lauterpacht J., dissenting).

[8] *Ibid.*, at 115 (Lauterpacht J., dissenting); *Certain Norwegian Loans* (*France* v. *Norway*), 1957 ICJ 9, 55 (Lauterpacht J., dissenting).

[9] See Yuval Shany, *Assessing the Effectiveness of International Courts* (New York: Oxford University Press, 2014), pp. 138–140.

[10] See also *Free Zones of Upper Savoy and the District of Gex*, 1929 PCIJ (ser A) (No. 22), at 12 (Order of 19 August 1929) ('the Court cannot, on the proposal of the Parties, depart from the terms of the Statute').

power), such a potential power does not contradict the proposition that the act of delegation attendant to the conferment of jurisdiction results in the parties irrevocably losing their *unilateral* decision-making power in relation to the dispute in question.

One possible justification for the different approach taken to a joint decision by the disputing parties to reach out-of-court settlements (following which the case is withdrawn from the court's docket), as compared to the response to self-judging clauses aimed at reaching the same result, is that the first method for disposition of the case does not harm the legitimacy of international court, since it does not typically purport to offer a competing determination of facts, interpretation of the law or application of the law to the facts. Hence, out-of-court settlements are not normally regarded as a challenge to the court's ultimate authority to perform its adjudicative function with respect to the case before it. Still, certain *ex ante* agreements by the disputing parties concerning the terms under which they undertake to jointly withdraw from the proceedings may also raise legitimacy questions, if they are deemed to interfere with the relevant court's foundational powers.[11]

A further example of the interplay between specific and foundational jurisdictional conditions involving questions of effectiveness

[11] See e.g. Treaty of Gulf of Maine Boundary Dispute Settlement (Canada/US), 29 March 1979, in force 20 November 1981, Art. 2, 20 ILM (1981) 1371:

> If for any reason, the Chamber referred to in article I has not been constituted in accordance with the provisions of this Treaty and the Special Agreement by the end of the sixth full calendar month after the date of entry into force of this Treaty either Party may, at any time prior to the constitution of the Chamber, terminate the Special Agreement .... In the event the Special Agreement is terminated, the Parties shall jointly notify the International Court of Justice that the proceedings under the Special Agreement are discontinued.

The compatibility of the agreement with the ICJ Statute has been *de facto* accepted by the Court, who chose to conduct itself in accordance with the wishes of the parties. Delimitation of the Maritime Boundary in the Gulf of Maine Area, 1982 ICJ 3, 10 (Constitution of Chamber) (Declaration by Judge Oda). This outcome has been strongly criticized by two of the Court's Judges, see *Ibid.*, at 11 (dissenting opinion of Judge Morozov) ('the sovereign right of the Court to carry out the election independently of the wishes of the Parties, by secret ballot in accordance with the provisions of the Statute and Rules of Court, has become meaningless'); *Ibid.*, at 12 (dissenting opinion of Judge Al-Khani) ('I find that the imposition of an unduly close time-limit for the Chamber's formation and of a particular composition renders the Court no longer master of its own acts ... Furthermore, it diminishes the prestige of the Court and is harmful to its dignity as the principal judicial organ of the United Nations').

can be found in the decision of the European Court of Human Rights (ECtHR) in *Loizidou* (2005), which examined the validity of the Turkish reservation to its declaration accepting the compulsory jurisdictional of the Court. In its decision on jurisdiction, the ECtHR held that a key condition appended to the Turkish declaration of acceptance of jurisdiction – Turkey's limitation of the *ratione loci* jurisdiction of the Court – runs contrary to the object and purpose of the European Convention on Human Rights (ECHR) and would weaken, if tolerated, the effectiveness of the Convention system:

> Such a system, which would enable States to qualify their consent under the optional clauses, would not only seriously weaken the role of the Commission and Court in the discharge of their functions but would also diminish the effectiveness of the Convention as a constitutional instrument of European public order (*ordre public*) . . . Moreover, where the Convention permits States to limit their acceptance under Article 25 (art. 25), there is an express stipulation to this effect . . . In the Court's view, having regard to the object and purpose of the Convention system as set out above, the consequences for the enforcement of the Convention and the achievement of its aims would be so far-reaching that a power to this effect should have been expressly provided for. However no such provision exists in either Article 25 or Article 46.[12]

It appears that the ECtHR understood its mission under the ECHR as primarily directed at the promotion of respect for human rights in Europe, and it therefore regarded the Turkish specific jurisdictional condition, which purported to exclude Northern Cyprus from the purview of the Court's jurisdiction, as incompatible with that mission. Put differently, the Court resorted to considerations of effectiveness – the ability of the Court to attain its norm-advancing goals[13] – when rejecting the permissibility of applying a specific jurisdictional condition (found in an instrument of unilateral acceptance of jurisdiction), limiting thereby the scope of jurisdiction set out in the Court's constitutive treaty.

We may note a critical difference between the approach taken by Judge Lauterpacht in his two dissenting opinions in *Norwegian Loans* and *Interhandel* and the approach of the ECtHR in *Loizidou*. Whereas for Lauterpacht the legal consequence of the inclusion of an

[12] *Loizidou* v. *Turkey*, 1995 Eur. Ct. H.R. (ser. A) (No. 310), para 75.
[13] See Shany, *Assessing the Effectiveness of International Courts*, pp. 14, 38–40.

impermissible condition in a specific jurisdictional instrument was the nullification of the instrument authorizing the court's exercise of jurisdiction,[14] the ECtHR held in *Loizidou* that the *ratione loci* condition could be severed from the rest of the declaration accepting the Court's jurisdiction and retained jurisdiction over the case.[15] This difference in approach may be explained, in part, by the suggestion that the legitimizing role of consent may be greater for some courts than for others. It may well be that courts serving a special legal regime, such as regional economic integration courts or human rights courts, prioritize their mission of upholding the substantive norms contained in their constitutive instruments over the need to strictly follow the principle of consent by insisting on obtaining clear and unequivocal manifestations of consent. Indeed, the movement towards conferring regime courts with compulsory jurisdiction through amendment of the constitutive instruments of international courts[16] (and the growing number of compromissory clauses conferring compulsory jurisdiction upon international courts)[17] suggests that states themselves place in some areas of their relations a lesser premium on consent and on their ability to withhold it. Instead, they seem to prefer the greater degree of effectiveness in dispute resolution and law enforcement that may be secured by conferring compulsory jurisdiction on international courts.

In addition, different international courts may require higher or lower degrees of consent to their jurisdiction in accordance with the unique legal and political context in which they operate. For example, one possible explanation for the reluctance by the ICJ to narrowly construe reservations to declarations of acceptance of its 'optional clause' is that such an approach might deter states from accepting the compulsory jurisdiction of the Court under any

[14] *Certain Norwegian Loans* (*France* v. *Norway*), 1957 ICJ 9, 57–59 (Lauterpacht J., dissenting); *Interhandel*, (*Switzerland* v. *US*), 1959 ICJ 6, 117 (Lauterpacht J., dissenting).

[15] *Loizidou*, note 12, at para 97.

[16] See Protocol No. 11 to the EC HR and Fundamental Freedoms, restructuring the control machinery established therein, 11 May 1994, in force 1 November 1998, ETS 155.

[17] See e.g. Daniel Lovric, *Deference to the Legislature in WTO Challenges to Legislation* (Alphen aan den Rijn: Kluwer Law International, 2010), p. 36; Sara McLaughlin Mitchell and Emilia Justyna Powell, *Domestic Law Goes Global: Legal Traditions and International Courts* (Cambridge: Cambridge University Press, 2011), pp. 179–180.

conditions. The withdrawal of the United States from the 'optional clause' system in the aftermath of the Court's controversial jurisdictional holding in *Nicaragua* serves for the Court as a cautionary tale about the costs of perceived jurisdictional overreaching in a legal–political environment that does take compulsory jurisdiction for granted.[18] At the same time, it may be speculated that the ECHR, which by 1995 already enjoyed acceptance of its compulsory jurisdiction by all its member states, was sufficiently confident in its perceived legitimacy and assessed the likelihood of a backlash against a bold assertion of foundational jurisdiction – such as withdrawal of declarations of acceptance – as relatively low.

Scope of jurisdiction and evaluation of judicial performance

I have suggested in the previous subsection that the delineation of the relationship between specific and foundational jurisdiction may have legitimacy and effectiveness implications, and may be determined based on such considerations. I will show in Parts II and III that this is also generally true of questions of jurisdiction and admissibility: they raise issues of legitimacy and effectiveness. Hence, when we evaluate courts as policy instruments and ask whether they are viewed as legitimate and effective, we should consider not only issues of perceived fairness, justice, goal attainment, and so forth, but also whether courts have been equipped with the necessary foundational and specific jurisdictional powers to function properly and to attain their goals.

For example, the ICC was created as a policy instrument intended to end impunity but has been equipped by limited personal jurisdiction, since, in the absence of a Security Council authorization, the Court may only try those individuals who hold the nationality of states that consented to the Court's jurisdiction or have allegedly committed crimes in the territory of such states.[19] In a world in which the Security Council rarely grants article 13 authorizations, and where states implicated in conflicts (with the exception of Africa, and perhaps

[18] See e.g. Tai-Heng Cheng, *When International Law Works: Realistic Idealism after 9/11 and the Global Recession* (New York: Oxford University Press, 2012), p. 173; Edward McWhinney and Paul Martin, *The International Court of Justice and the Western Tradition of International Law* (Dordrecht: Martinus Nijhoff Publishers, 1987), pp. 105–108.

[19] ICC Statute, Arts. 12 and 13.

also Latin America) tend not to consent to the Court's jurisdiction, the Court inevitably engages in a selective application of international justice (thus raising legitimacy and other concerns)[20] and its ability to realize its policy goal may consequently be rather limited (raising effectiveness concerns).[21]

In the same vein, expectations that the ICJ would play a central role in the maintenance of international peace and security must be understood in the light of the strong consent requirement that underpins the exercise of ICJ jurisdiction and the propensity of states to reject binding third-party settlement in cases involving important national interests.[22] This implies that the Court's ability to attain the goal of preventing and defusing the most volatile international conflicts is limited.[23] Furthermore, the ICJ's inability to hear disputes involving non-state actors, due to its state-centric jurisdictional configuration, renders it less and less relevant to contemporary international relations, in which states are not as important as they used to be, and puts its legitimacy in question.[24]

At the same time, it would be too limiting to regard jurisdictional powers as a permanent attribute that predetermines judicial performance. Acceptance of jurisdiction of an international court by state parties or other potential litigants may be regarded as a vote of confidence in the court indicative of satisfaction with its record of performance. Hence, the stable though quite limited flow of cases to the ICJ over the years,[25] and the very modest increase in the number

[20] See e.g. Rowland J V Cole, 'Africa's Relationship with the International Criminal Court: More Political than Legal' (2014) 14 MELBOURNE J. OF INT'L LAW 670, 691–692; Pierre Hazan, *Justice in a Time of War: The True Story behind the International Criminal Tribunal for the Former Yugoslavia* (James Thomas Snyder, trans., College Station: Texas A&M University Press, 2004), p. 200.

[21] See Shany, *Assessing the Effectiveness of International Courts*, pp. 75–83.

[22] See e.g. Peter Malanczuk, *Akehurst's Modern Introduction to International Law*, 7th revised edn. (London: Routledge, 1997), p. 302; Stanley Michalak, *A Primer in Power Politics* (Wilmington, DE: Scholarly Resources Inc., 2001), p. 27; Ram Prakash Anand, 'Enhancing the Acceptability of Compulsory Procedure of International Dispute Resolution' (2001) 5 MAX PLANCK YB UN LAW 16.

[23] See Yuval Shany, 'No Longer A Weak Department of Power? Reflections on the Emergence of a New International Judiciary' (2009) 20 EUR. J. INT'L L. 73, 80.

[24] See Ruti G Teitel, *Humanity's Law* (New York: Oxford University Press, 2011), p. 171; Antônio Augusto Cançado Trindade, *The Access of Individuals to International Justice* (New York: Oxford University Press, 2011), pp. 113–114.

[25] See Rotem Giladi and Yuval Shany, 'The International Court of Justice', in Shany, *Assessing the Effectiveness of International Courts*, pp. 161, 175–176.

of optional clause declarations,[26] are probably reflective both of the limited propensity of states to consent to the jurisdiction of the ICJ and of the ongoing appreciation of the Court's utility, at least in some circumstances. By contrast, the expansion of the jurisdictional powers of European Court of Human Rights during the 1990s following the conclusion of Protocol 11, which coincided with a sharp rise in the membership in the ECHR, can be understood at least partly as a positive evaluation of the Court's performance and broad acceptance of its legitimacy.

In short, jurisdictional powers tend to constrain the performance of international courts, and affect their perceived utility and legitimacy. Yet performance or perceptions of performance may support or hinder reforms in the jurisdictional configuration of international courts. Thus, a 'feedback loop' exists between jurisdiction on the one hand, and legitimacy and effectiveness on the other hand:[27] The success of the Court in utilizing its existing jurisdiction may lead to its investment with more jurisdiction, and its failures may lead to narrowing down of its jurisdiction.

[26] In 1992 there were 56 Optional Clause Declarations; their number has increased to 70 by 2014 (including 24 new declarations and the withdrawal or expiration of ten old declarations).

[27] See Shany, *Assessing the Effectiveness of International Courts*, p. 96.

4

The role of admissibility in the exercise of judicial power

The concept of admissibility

If jurisdiction reflects legal power – that is, the power to adjudicate a dispute – then I propose to treat rules of admissibility as pertaining to the terms permitting an international court to decline to exercise its legal powers. In other words, international courts may be authorized not only to decide a legal case, but also to decide not to decide it.

The authorization to decide whether to adjudicate a dispute, which falls under the jurisdiction of an international court – that is, whether or not to find a case inadmissible – may be explicitly stated in the court's constitutive instruments or derived implicitly therefrom. To the extent that it emanates from the same legal instrument investing the international court with foundational jurisdiction or from the specific instrument representing the consent of the parties to invoke the specific jurisdiction of the court, the authorization to decline jurisdiction enjoys the same legal status as the authorization to exercise jurisdiction.

For example, article 53 of the International Criminal Court (ICC) Statute, a constitutive instrument containing a general grant of jurisdiction, instructs the Court to review under certain circumstances a decision by the Prosecutor not to proceed with a prosecution where such a course of action would not be in the interests of justice.[1]

[1] The ICC Statute, Art. 53:

> 1 … In deciding whether to initiate an investigation, the Prosecutor shall consider whether: (a) The information available to the Prosecutor provides a reasonable basis to believe that a crime within the jurisdiction of the Court has been or is being committed; (b) The case is or would be admissible under

This amounts to authorizing the Prosecutor and the Court's Pre-Trial Chamber to decide whether or not to exercise the legal power to adjudicate international crimes invested in the Court due to the existence of certain circumstances, which would render adjudication undesirable.

Another example of an admissibility provision can be found in the United Nations Convention on the Law of the Sea (UNCLOS), an instrument establishing a new Court (the International Tribunal for the Law of the Sea – ITLOS) and containing a compromissory clause (article 287) referring cases to either ITLOS or other adjudicatory bodies (including the International Court of Justice – ICJ). Article 294 of the UNCLOS reads as follows:

> 1. A court or tribunal provided for in article 287 to which an application is made in respect of a dispute referred to in article 297 shall determine at the request of a party, or may determine *proprio motu*, whether the claim constitutes an abuse of legal process or whether *prima facie* it is well founded. If the court or tribunal determines that the claim constitutes an abuse of legal process or is *prima facie* unfounded, it shall take no further action in the case.[2]

As will be discussed in the ensuing pages, abuse of process and ill-founded claims may be regarded as admissibility rules. This is because they do not negate the very grant of authority to adjudicate conferred on one of the dispute-settlement procedures listed in article 287 of the UNCLOS, but rather allow them to decline jurisdiction due to the impropriety of exercising their adjudicatory powers under certain circumstances. Here too, it may be argued that since the conditions underlying inadmissibility decisions are found in the instrument establishing the UNCLOS's dispute-settlement procedures and include a *proprio motu* procedure for review of admissibility

article 17; and (c) Taking into account the gravity of the crime and the interests of victims, there are nonetheless substantial reasons to believe that an investigation would not serve the interests of justice . . . . .3 (a) At the request of the State making a referral under article 14 or the Security Council under article 13, paragraph (b), the Pre-Trial Chamber may review a decision of the Prosecutor under paragraph 1 or 2 not to proceed and may request the Prosecutor to reconsider that decision. (b) In addition, the Pre-Trial Chamber may, on its own initiative, review a decision of the Prosecutor not to proceed if it is based solely on paragraph 1 (c) or 2 (c). In such a case, the decision of the Prosecutor shall be effective only if confirmed by the Pre-Trial Chamber.

[2] UNCLOS, Art. 294.

of the case, they cannot be derogated from by the disputing parties. The same considerations that explain the inability of the disputing parties to change the scope of an international court's foundational jurisdiction, or to ignore not-to-be-waived jurisdictional conditions attached to such foundational jurisdiction, also support the conclusion that the disputing parties cannot detract from the powers to decline jurisdiction granted to the court in its constitutive instrument.

Another possible source of rules on admissibility may be found in general rules of international law governing the exercise of judicial power. Some international courts have often operated on the basis of the assumption that their constitutive instruments were not designed to exclude the application of these general rules. In *Eastern Carelia*, for example, the Permanent Court of International Justice (PCIJ) took the view that its legal power to issue an advisory opinion on a question relating to a concrete interstate dispute was subject to the principle of state consent, which the Court identified as a fundamental principle of international law and whose circumvention the Court deemed to be improper.[3] In the same vein, one can understand the ICJ's decision in *Monetary Gold* to decline to hear a case where the vital issue at stake concerned the responsibility of a third state, as another application of the proposition that it would be improper to exercise jurisdiction if such exercise runs contrary to the principle that state consent is needed for international adjudication of its legal rights.[4]

Another example of a rule of admissibility derived from general international law can be found in *Rights of Minorities in Upper Silesia* (PCIJ 1928), where the Court held that its jurisdiction would become inoperative 'in those exceptional cases in which the dispute which States may desire to refer to the Court would fall within the exclusive jurisdiction reserved to some other authority'.[5] Arguably, it is the general principle of law of *pacta sunt servanda,* which counselled in the circumstances of the case against the exercise of jurisdiction by

[3] *Eastern Carelia,* 1923 PCIJ Ser. B, No. 5, at 27.

[4] *Monetary Gold Removed from Rome in 1943* (*Italy* v. *France and others*), 1954 ICJ 19, 32 ('To adjudicate upon the international responsibility of Albania without her consent would run counter to a well-established principle of international law embodied in the Court's Statute, namely, that the Court can only exercise jurisdiction over a State with its consent').

[5] *Rights of Minorities in Upper Silesia* (*Germany* v. *Poland*), 1928 PCIJ Ser. A, No. 15, at 23.

the Court in contravention to an agreement to adjudicate the case elsewhere.[6]

Another source of admissibility rules claimed by several international courts and commentators is the inherent power of international courts. According to this approach, international courts have an inherent right to decline to exercise jurisdiction when to do so would undermine the court's judicial function (i.e. undermine its legitimacy) or be devoid of purpose (lack effectiveness). Arguably, the ICJ's decisions in *Northern Cameroons*[7] and *Nuclear Tests*[8] – both discussed in Part III – fall into this category.

Still, as I discuss in the ensuing pages, some international courts, especially those operating in a specialized field of law, have taken a different approach to the question of the applicability of rules of admissibility deriving from their so-called inherent powers. For example, the World Trade Organization (WTO) Appellate Body held in *Mexico-Soft Drinks* that the WTO dispute-settlement panels are bound to exercise the jurisdiction invested with them, and may not decline it in the absence of an explicit mandate to that effect.[9]

As far as I can tell, it is not possible to find examples of admissibility rules derived from a specific jurisdiction instrument, conferring on international courts a power to decline to adjudicate that go beyond any powers that they already possess under their constitutive instruments.[10] The reason for this is that the granting of specific

[6] *Cf. ibid.*, at 25 ('If, in a special case, the Respondent has, by an express declaration, indicated his desire to obtain a decision on the merits and his intention to abstain from raising the question of jurisdiction, it seems clear that he cannot, later on in the proceedings, go back upon that declaration').

[7] *Northern Cameroons*, 1963 ICJ 15, 29 ('There are *inherent* limitations on the exercise of the judicial function which the Court, as a court of justice, can never ignore').

[8] *Nuclear Tests* (*Australia* v. *France*), 1974 ICJ 253, 271 ('The Court therefore sees no reason to allow the continuance of proceedings which it knows are bound to be fruitless').

[9] *Mexico – Tax Measures on Soft Drinks and Other Beverages*, Report of the AB of 6 March 2006, WTO Doc. WT/DS308/AB/R, at xix–xx ('In our view, it does not necessarily follow, however, from the existence of these inherent adjudicative powers that, once jurisdiction has been validly established, WTO panels would have the authority to decline to rule on the entirety of the claims that are before them in a dispute').

[10] Specific jurisdiction instruments may confirm, however, the general legal powers of international courts under their constitutive instruments, including the power to declare the case inadmissible. See Special Agreement to Submit Guatemala's Territorial, Insular and Maritime Claim to the International Court of Justice

consent with respect to a dispute that has already arisen implies a belief by the disputing parties that the case could and should be adjudicated by an authorized international court. As for the reverse situation – a specific jurisdiction instrument purporting to limit an international court's power to declare a case inadmissible pursuant to its constitutive instruments – the same reasons that operate to limit the disputing parties' ability to stipulate on the scope of foundational jurisdiction would appear to resist stipulations against admissibility rules found in the respective constitutive instrument. This is especially the case when the parties waive admissibility rules, which are designed to protect the proper judicial function of the international court in question.[11] For similar reasons, the court may presume that the parties did not intend to agree to stipulate on the legal powers included in its constitutive instrument, including its power to hold cases inadmissible, which are necessary to maintain its proper judicial function.[12]

Hence, one can understand the decision of the PCIJ in *Eastern Carelia* to declare the request for advisory opinion inadmissible[13] either as indicative of its view that the Council of the League that referred the question to the Court did not have the legal power to detract from the Court's inherent powers (presumably emanating from its Statute) to decline jurisdiction, or that the Council did not intend for the Court to exercise jurisdiction under conditions which it would deem to be improper and inexpedient.[14]

(Belize and Guatemala), 8 December 2008, Art. 3(5), www.oas.org/sap/peacefund/PeaceMissions/SpecialAgreementBetweenBelizeandGuatemala.pdf.

[11] See *Northern Cameroons,* 1963 ICJ 15, at 29 ('The Court itself, and not the parties, must be the guardian of the Court's judicial integrity'). *Cf. Free Zones,* 1932 PCIJ (Ser A/B) No. 46, at 161–162 (the Court opining that a Special Agreement subjecting a judgment to the approval of the parties is incompatible with the Statute and the role of the PCIJ as a Court of Justice).

[12] *Cf. ibid.,* at 153 ('While it is certain that the Parties, being free to dispose of their rights, might have embodied, in the negotiations contemplated in Article 1, paragraph 2, of the Special Agreement, and might also in any future negotiations embody in their agreement any provisions they might desire ... it in no way follows that the Court enjoys the same freedom. Such freedom, being contrary to the proper function of the Court, could, in any case, only be enjoyed by it if such freedom resulted from a clear and explicit provision which is not to be found in the Special Agreement').

[13] *Eastern Carelia,* 1923 PCIJ (ser. B) (No. 5), at 27–28.

[14] *Ibid.,* at 29 ('It is with regret that the Court, the Russian government having refused their concurrence, finds itself unable to pursue the investigation which, as the terms of the Council's Resolution had foreshadowed, would require the consent and co-operation of both parties').

The link between admissibility, legitimacy and effectiveness

The link between rules of admissibility and judicial propriety and expediency (or legitimacy and effectiveness) is quite straightforward. The notion of jurisdiction defines the legal powers that may be exercised by an international court in order to attain its goals, and, as explained earlier, perceptions of goal attainment influence the legitimacy it enjoys in the eyes of relevant constituencies. There may be occasions, however, when the exercise of jurisdiction would be undesirable from the viewpoint of an international court, since it would not advance its goals, or would require it to deviate from what it regards as its proper judicial function. Hence, international courts may prefer to avoid to adjudicate certain cases, and the rules of admissibility provide them with a legally valid method to decline jurisdiction in appropriate cases.

A classic example of declining jurisdiction for reasons related to considerations of effectiveness and legitimacy is the PCIJ'S opinion in the above-mentioned *Eastern Carelia* case – the only advisory opinion to date in which the World Court declined a request for an advisory opinion for reasons of inadmissibility (as opposed to lack of jurisdiction, which led to dismissal of one case by the ICJ).[15] In its decision, the Court cited lack of consent and cooperation by a relevant state (Russia) as a factor relating to both the propriety and expediency of its acceptance of jurisdiction. Although state consent is not a prerequisite for the issuance of advisory opinions, the Court felt that in the circumstances of the case, which were intimately related to an interstate dispute, it should not exercise its legal powers vis-à-vis a state that was not even a member of the League of Nations at the time. This is because the exercise of jurisdiction without Russia's consent would put the PCIJ in conflict with fundamental principles of international law such as the sovereign equality of states and its corollary that no state can be compelled to submit its disputes to a pacific dispute-settlement procedure without its consent.[16] In addition, the Court also opined that it would be 'inexpedient' to proceed without Russia's cooperation since the Court's ability to establish the facts underlying the dispute would be seriously compromised under such conditions. The Court was of the view that answering a

[15] *Legality of the Use by a State of Nuclear Weapons in Armed Conflict*, 1996 ICJ 66.
[16] *Eastern Carelia*, 1923 PCIJ (ser. B) (No. 5), at 27.

legal question without a solid factual basis would be not only be ineffective, but also illegitimate, as it would deviate from 'the essential rules guiding its activities as a 'Court of Justice'.[17]

Another example of a rule of admissibility invoked by the ICJ for reasons relating to considerations of effectiveness and legitimacy can be found in *Northern Cameroons.* In this case, the Court decided not to exercise its jurisdiction over a dispute raising a question of an inoperative or moot nature, holding that 'for the Court to proceed further in the case would not, in its opinion, be a proper discharge of its duties'.[18] Arguably, the application's lack of a practical purpose might amount to a wasteful utilization of judicial resource; it might also portray the Court in a negative light as a useless institution. According to the judgment, this legitimacy concern established a 'duty to safeguard the judicial process'.[19] In such cases, further discussed in Part III, where the exercise of jurisdiction over a dispute was deemed counterproductive, protecting the Court's judicial function may require it to decline jurisdiction.

[17] *Ibid.*, at 29. [18] *Northern Cameroons,* 1963 ICJ 15, at 38. [19] *Ibid.*, at 38.

5

The conflicting considerations governing the review of jurisdiction and admissibility

Conflicting policy considerations

The discussion in the preceding segments of this part suggests that international judges appraising their power of jurisdiction over cases submitted to them and reviewing the admissibility of such cases may confront a number of conflicting considerations pertaining to the values and interests of the mandate provides, the disputing parties and other constituencies (such as the general public). Furthermore, two of the main institutional considerations employed by international courts – effectiveness and legitimacy – may also point on occasion in opposite directions.

Indeed, case selection represents an important area in regard to which strong tensions between competing interests and values may arise. The advancement of the goals set for the court by its mandate providers may militate in favour of focusing judicial efforts on a specific category of cases, most likely to promote the normative agendas and policies consistent with such goals. This may support, through the combined application of jurisdictional and admissibility rules, expanding the court's judicial business in some directions, and excluding from its purview cases whose goal-attainment potential is more limited. To illustrate, for reasons relating to its mission to fight impunity, the International Criminal Court (ICC) may embrace a broad understanding of article 12(3) of its Statute – the jurisdictional provision governing case referrals by states not parties to the Statute – including political entities whose claim for statehood status is uncertain.[1] At the same time, the Court may

[1] For a discussion, see Yaël Ronen, 'ICC Jurisdiction over Acts Committed in the Gaza Strip: Article 12(3) of the ICC Statute and Non-State Entities' (2010) 8 JICJ 3; Yuval

narrowly construe the notion of gravity under article 17(1)(d) and declare inadmissible cases resulting in relatively small numbers of casualties, so that it can concentrate on the 'most serious crimes'.[2] To the extent that the fine-tuning of the Court's legal powers through the interpretation and application of its jurisdiction and admissibility provisions is indeed driven by a goal-attainment perspective, the process is expected to be dominated by teleological considerations, and will inevitably prioritize the expectations of some constituencies (interested in the outcome of cases falling under the selected criteria) over other constituencies (interested in the outcome of cases falling outside the selected criteria).

At the same time, legitimacy concerns – that is, the need to preserve the image of international courts in the eyes of relevant constituencies as rule of law institutions who are themselves governed by law – may restrict the court's freedom of manoeuvre in pursuit of a general normative agenda (such as promoting international peace and security or ending impunity). This is especially so when the agenda is not clearly spelled out in the instruments containing jurisdictional and admissibility provisions, or requires a different treatment of cases raising similar legal issues (albeit in different factual contexts). Thus, whereas effectiveness considerations may encourage the flexible and teleological interpretation of jurisdictional and admissibility provisions, legitimacy concerns may pull in a different direction and push international courts towards textualism and formalism (e.g. insisting on clear proof of consent before assuming jurisdiction even though this may deprive the Court of a chance to apply the law to the case in a manner conducive to promoting its normative agenda).

Even where the needs of goal attainment would support overextending or under-reading the letter of the provisions governing jurisdictional and admissibility, doing so may result in erosion of the determinacy of the legal standard in question, thus reducing

Shany, 'In Defense of Functional Interpretation of Article 12(3) of the Rome Statute', 329.

[2] ICC Statute, preamble. For a discussion of the Court's gravity jurisprudence, see *Situation in the Democratic Republic of the Congo*, Judgment of 13 July 2006 on the Prosecutor's Appeal against the Decision of Pre-Trial Chamber I entitled 'Decision on the Prosecutor's Application for Warrants of Arrest, Article 58' (in re Bosco Ntaganda), Case No. ICC-01/04–169, at paras 69–82 (13 July 2006), available at www.icc-cpi.int/iccdocs/doc/doc183559.pdf; Margaret M. deGuzman, 'The International Criminal Court's Gravity Jurisprudence at Ten' (2013) 12 Wash. U. Global Stud. L. Rev. 475.

the perceived legitimacy of the decision to adjudicate or not to adjudicate the case.[3] Furthermore, by moving away from strictly textual interpretations, there is a greater chance that legal provisions on jurisdiction and admissibility may be construed across cases in an inconsistent manner so as to accommodate unique case-selection considerations.[4] In such cases, the coherence, and consequently the fairness, of the court's approach may be open to challenge.[5] Finally, to the extent that teleological interpretation and application of jurisdictional and admissibility provisions impinges on basic principle of international law, which may also be reflected in the Court's constitutive instruments – for example, consent or *pacta sunt servanda* – additional legitimacy concerns are raised (potentially couched in the Frankian notion of adherence).[6] Such concerns about loss of legitimacy resulting out of a deviation from basic principle of international law probably led the International Court of Justice (ICJ) judges to reject Judge Alvarez's call in *Anglo-Iranian* to construe the ICJ Statute as permitting compulsory jurisdiction in cases relating to norms comprising part of 'new international law'.[7] Put differently, the Court's insistence on maintaining the formal jurisdictional condition of consent was reason enough to reject the radical teleological reading of the Statute proposed by Judge Alvarez that sought to do away with the fundamental principle of what he referred to as 'classic international law'.

The decision whether or not to prioritize regime goals over legitimacy concerns appears to be context dependent. While the ICJ, whose business depends to a large extent on voluntary submissions of disputes by states, may be particularly sensitive to their expectations that its jurisdiction will strictly remain within the scope of the powers delegated to it, other international courts operating on the basis of compulsory jurisdiction may be less sensitive to such concerns. For example, the Court of Justice of the European Union (CJEU) decided in two decisions issued before the

[3] See Thomas M Franck, *The Power of Legitimacy among Nations* (New York, Oxford: Oxford University Press, 1990), pp. 50–66.

[4] See the discussions in Part II of the series of decisions issued after 1993 involving the legal status of Yugoslavia.

[5] See Franck, *The Power of Legitimacy among Nations*, pp. 150–182.

[6] *Ibid.*, at 183–194.

[7] *Anglo-Iranian Oil Co.* (*UK* v. *Iran*), 1952 ICJ 93, 130–134 (dissenting opinion of Judge Alvarez).

conclusion of the EU Treaty – *Le Verts* and *Parliament* v. *Council* – to confer upon the European Parliament a right to sue and be sued in annulment actions beyond the jurisdictional provisions of the Treaty of Rome, as they stood at the time.[8] The Court suggested that such a legal development is necessary to maintain the balance between European institutions – that is, to advance the goal of regime support.[9] In the circumstances of these cases, it appears as if the accountability-enhancing dimension of the decisions, and the growing political consensus around the need to empower the Parliament (as a way to reduce the democratic deficit of the EU) conferred legitimacy on the outcomes reached which has offset any loss of legitimacy incurred by the act of judicial legislation *de facto* resorted to by the Court.

Another example of the need to mediate between the adjudicators' interest in advancing their regime goals, which tends to pull towards a teleological construction of jurisdictional and admissibility provisions, and their fidelity to the explicit language used in the constitutive instruments which delineate their powers can be found in the admissibility decision issued by an ICSID arbitration tribunal in *Tokios Tokeles.* This case involved an investment in the Ukraine by a Lithuanian company controlled by Ukrainian shareholders, and the question it raised was whether given its particular features the 'foreign investment' in question fell under the jurisdiction of ICSID arbitration. The majority on the tribunal (comprising, interestingly enough, the two party-appointed arbitrators) argued that their powers to decline jurisdiction are constrained by the text of the jurisdiction-conferring instruments, which did not create an exception for foreign investments controlled by local investors:

> We find no basis in the BIT or the Convention to set aside the Contracting Parties' agreed definition of corporate nationality with respect to investors or either party in favour of a test based on the nationality of the controlling shareholder.[10]

The President of the Tribunal, Prosper Weil, took the opposite view and opted for a teleological reading of the relevant jurisdictional

[8] C294-83 *Le Verts* v. *Parliament* [1986] ECR 1339; C-70/88 Parliament *v.* Council, [1990] ECR I-2041.

[9] See Yuval Shany, *Assessing the Effectiveness of International Courts* (New York: Oxford University Press, 2014), pp. 43–44.

[10] *Tokios Tokelés* v. *Ukraine,* ICSID Case No. ARB/02/18, Decision on Jurisdiction of 29 April 2004, at para 52.

provisions of the ICSID Conventions: 'To maintain, as the Decision does that "the origin of the capital is not relevant" ... runs counter to the object and purpose of the whole ICSID system'.[11] Note, however, that the conflicting positions of the arbitrators in this case cannot be boiled down to a choice between considerations of effectiveness and legitimacy, as Weil couched his support of a teleological approach focusing on the goals of the ICSID regime also in the need to preserve the integrity of the system.[12] This position is consistent with the insight that considerations of effectiveness and legitimacy are often interrelated – that is, that a more effective international court enjoys higher degrees of legitimacy in the eyes of its constituencies, and that a more legitimate court is better situated than one perceived as less legitimate to attain its goals and to perform its functions in an effective manner.[13] In other words, international courts must retain a minimal amount of both effectiveness and legitimacy in order to continue to operate. It is rather a question of assigning relative weights to the two values and engaging in certain trade-offs between them in those cases where they point international courts to move in different directions. Arguably, for each international court a different point of equilibrium would be optimal; moreover, this point of equilibrium may vary over time and across different types of cases.

To be sure, considerations of legitimacy and effectiveness, potentially translating themselves into different methods of interpretation, do not necessary stand in conflict with one another, since the plain language of jurisdictional and admissibility provisions found in the relevant constitutive instruments is often closely aligned with the broader goals of the international court in question. For example, when opting to construe the complementarity test in a manner which treats inaction (lack of investigation or prosecution) as an irrefutable indication of unwillingness or inability to prosecute, the ICC argued that to hold otherwise would be

> not only irreconcilable with the wording of the provision, but [also] in conflict with a purposive interpretation of the Statute. The aim of the Rome Statute is 'to put an end to impunity' ... This object and purpose of

[11] *Ibid.*, at para 19 (dissenting opinion of Prosper Weil). [12] *Ibid.*, at para 25.
[13] See the discussions in Shany, *Assessing the Effectiveness of International Courts*, p. 158.

the Statute would come to naught were the said interpretation of article 17(1) of the Statute as proposed by the Appellant to prevail.[14]

Institutional concerns

An additional factor, which further complicates the decision what approach to embrace in construing jurisdictional and admissibility provisions and how to engage in trade-offs between competing values and interests, is the idiosyncratic institutional interest of the court in question, which can militate in favour or against accepting jurisdiction in a specific case. Thus, for example, some commentators have rather cynically attributed the propensity of arbitral tribunals to retain jurisdiction to the financial incentives associated with prolonging adjudication and conducting hearings on the merits.[15] More generally, it may be presumed that an international court may be interested in hearing a case in order to increase its caseload or its perceived relevance to certain policy problem area. Alternatively, an international court may be inclined to refrain from accepting jurisdiction over too many cases, resulting in the overcrowding of its docket, or from adjudicating politically sensitive cases which may harm the Court's reputation or lead to unhealthy splits among the judges.

Thus, Sean Murphy suggested a reading of the ICJ's controversial decision in *Nicaragua* as an attempt by the Court to 'expand the reach of its power', as well as an attempt by the Court to reposition itself in the world of international institutions:

> Having stood up to the United States in the *Nicaragua* case, the Court became a hero to the states of the developing world, and ushered in a period of increased activity on its docket.[16]

[14] *Prosecutor* v. *Katanga*, ICC Case No. ICC-01/04–01/07 OA 8, Judgment of the Appeals Chamber on the Admissibility of the Case, 25 September 2009, at para 79.

[15] See e.g. Gus Van Harten and Martin Loughlin, 'Investment Treaty Arbitration as a Species of Global Administrative Law' (2006) 17 *EJIL* 121, 148; Cecilia Olivet, The Dark Side of Investment Agreements (December 2011), www.tni.org/sites/www.tni.org/files/the_dark_side_of_investment_treaties-final.pdf.

[16] Sean D Murphy, 'The United States and the International Court of Justice', in Cesare Romano (ed.), *The Sword and the Scales: The United States and International Courts and Tribunals* (Cambridge: Cambridge University Press, 2008), pp. 46, 97.

One may speculate that the advisory opinion on *Kosovo*[17] marks an opposite approach by the Court to its scope of jurisdictional power, which was nonetheless influenced by institutional considerations. Arguably, the choice of a narrow as possible reading of the Court's jurisdiction over the request helped the Court to avoid dealing with the politically explosive matter of remedial secession.

Parts II and III will offer other examples for the manner in which competing policies, considerations and constituency expectations may be factored in decisions on jurisdiction and admissibility. Such examples underscore the interplay between power invested in courts and discretion on how to use such power – overtly (as is the case in many decisions on admissibility) or covertly (as it is in decisions on the interpretation of jurisdictional provisions and the scope of powers to decline jurisdiction for reasons of inadmissibility).

[17] *Accordance with International Law of the Unilateral Declaration of Independence in Respect of Kosovo*, 2010 ICJ 403.

Part II

Jurisdictional decisions of international courts

6

Jurisdiction *in abstracto* and *in concreto*

Jurisdictional authorizations and conditions

Once an international court has been established, it is endowed with jurisdiction *in abstracto* – that is, it has obtained a general power to adjudicate certain categories of cases. Indeed, the foundational jurisdictional provisions, found in the constitutive instruments establishing the relevant international courts, include a definition of the key features characterizing the disputes or situations which the court is authorized to adjudicate (jurisdiction *ratione personae, ratione materiae, ratione temporis, ratione loci*), as well as any jurisdictional conditions limiting the court's power to exercise jurisdiction under certain circumstances (such as when domestic remedies were not exhausted or when parallel proceedings are pending before another international court).

The definition of the prescribed jurisdictional boundaries and conditions is supplemented, at times, with general international law norms, which provides content and contexts to the term used. For example, the International Criminal Court (ICC) Office of the Prosecutor resorted in 2012 to general international law (and specifically, to United Nations law) in order to determine whether Palestine is a state, and thus authorized to invoke its jurisdiction *ratione personae*.[1] In addition, the International Court of Justice (ICJ) has resorted on more than one occasion to customary international law governing exhaustion of domestic remedies in order to

[1] International Court of Justice, Office of the Prosecutor, Situation in Palestine, 3 April 2012, paras 5–7.

limit the scope of the jurisdictional title conferred upon it by 'optional clause' declarations or compromissory clauses.[2]

Traditionally, the constitutive instruments of international courts established the consent of the parties to the adjudication to a specific case or a category of cases as the most important precondition for the exercise of jurisdiction.[3] Still, following the increased success of some international courts in attracting a critical mass of *ex ante* acceptances of their jurisdiction (e.g. in the form of 'optional clause' declarations)[4] and with the rise of international courts endowed with compulsory jurisdictions as part of their foundational jurisdiction, the centrality of consent as a jurisdictional condition has declined.

Significantly, jurisdictional authorizations bestowed upon international courts are not always uniform in scope, and different prospective parties may authorize the exercising of judicial power over different categories of cases. Through instruments expressing their consent to adjudication, where such consent is required, or, where possible, through the exercise of their implicit power to stipulate upon those powers of international courts that are dispositive in nature, potential parties to adjudication can specifically tailor the Court's scope of jurisdiction and exclude from it certain categories of disputes, which may otherwise fall within the Court's jurisdictional powers. Moreover, where the international court's constitutive instruments so permit, explicitly or implicitly, the parties may agree to expand its scope of jurisdiction.

Hence, for example, it is common for parties concluding agreements referring future disputes to the ICJ to limit the jurisdiction *ratione temporis* emanating from their consent to disputes arising after a certain date,[5] or to introduce certain jurisdictional conditions, such

2 See e.g. *Interhandel* (*Switzerland* v. *US*), 1959 ICJ 6, 27; *Elettronica Sicula S.p.A.* (ELSI) (*USA* v. *Italy*), 1989 ICJ 15, 42.

3 See e.g. ICJ Statute, art. 36; UNCLOS, art. 287.

4 See e.g. declarations accepting the compulsory jurisdiction of the Inter-American Court of Human Rights, pursuant to ACHR, art. 62. Currently, 19 out of the 22 member states to the Convention have accepted the Court's compulsory jurisdiction.

5 See e.g. article 27 of the European Convention for the Peaceful Settlement of Disputes, Strasbourg, 29 April 1957, in force 30 April 1958, art. 1, ETS 23, which excludes from the scope of consent to ICJ jurisdiction 'disputes relating to facts or situations prior to the entry into force of this Convention between the parties to the dispute'. This provision was relied upon by the Court to reach the conclusion that it has no jurisdiction over a dispute between Liechtenstein and Germany arising from post-World War Two property confiscations. *Certain Property* (*Liechtenstein* v. *Germany*), 2005 ICJ 6, 27.

as the need to exhaust other international dispute settlement procedures before referring disputes to ICJ adjudication.[6] Other examples of stipulation on the jurisdiction of an international tribunal can be found in the opting out arrangements introduced in articles 25 and 26 of the International Centre for Settlement of Investment Disputes (ICSID) Convention, allowing member states to exclude from the Centre's scope of jurisdiction certain classes of investment disputes or to require exhaustion of domestic remedies prior to the initiation of ICSID arbitration.[7] Such opt-out provisions can be regarded either as permissible limits placed on the member states' consent to adjudication or as specific jurisdictional arrangements deviating from the terms of foundational jurisdiction normally provided for under the ICSID Convention.

Note, however, that deviations from foundational jurisdiction may also take place with a view to expanding the jurisdiction of international courts. Indeed, some constitutive instruments explicitly allow the parties to agree to expand the foundational jurisdiction of the relevant international court beyond its ordinary scope of jurisdiction or to remove one of the preconditions to the exercise of jurisdiction. For example, the ICSID Convention authorizes the parties to a dispute to agree to extend the jurisdiction *ratione personae* of the Centre to cases involving juridical persons having the nationality of the host

[6] See e.g. art. 22 of the Convention on the Elimination of All Forms of Racial Discrimination, 21 December 1965, in force 4 January 1969, 660 UNTS 195, which the ICJ construed in *Application of CERD* as introducing a requirement to attempt to settle the dispute through negotiations and/or the Convention's own dispute settlement procedures prior to submission of the case to the ICJ. *Application of the International Convention on the Elimination of All Forms of Racial Discrimination* (*Georgia* v. *Russian Federation*), 2011 ICJ 70, 128–130.

[7] ICSID Convention. art. 25(4) reads:

> Any Contracting State may, at the time of ratification, acceptance or approval of this Convention or at any time thereafter, notify the Centre of the class or classes of disputes which it would or would not consider submitting to the jurisdiction of the Centre. The Secretary General shall forthwith transmit such notification to all Contracting 18 Convention States. Such notification shall not constitute the consent required by paragraph (1).

Art. 26 reads: 'Consent of the parties to arbitration under this Convention shall, unless otherwise stated, be deemed consent to such arbitration to the exclusion of any other remedy. A Contracting State may require the exhaustion of local administrative or judicial remedies as a condition of its consent to arbitration under this Convention'. Seven member states currently have valid art. 25(4) declarations, and two have valid art. 26 declarations. ICSID Doc. ICSID/8-D.

state whom 'because of foreign control, the parties have agreed should be treated as a national of another Contracting State for the purposes of this Convention'.[8] Another example of the potential of specific jurisdictional instruments to stipulate on foundational jurisdiction in a manner resulting in expansion of jurisdiction or removal of jurisdictional conditions can be found in the *dicta* used by the ICJ in the Elettronica Sicula S.p.A. (ELSI) case, dealing with the ability of the parties to waive their right to have domestic remedies exhausted before ICJ adjudication:

> The Chamber has no doubt that the parties to a treaty can therein either agree that the local remedies rule shall not apply to claims based on alleged breaches of that treaty; or confirm that it shall apply.[9]

The ability of the disputing parties to stipulate on the foundational jurisdiction of international courts is, however, not unlimited, and the Courts' constitutive instruments may explicitly or implicitly prohibit certain stipulations. For example, the combined effect of the prohibition of reservations under the Rome Statute and the possibility for a 7-year opt-out from ICC jurisdiction over war crimes is that member states cannot stipulate on the Court's foundational jurisdiction over crimes of genocide and crimes against humanity.[10] Furthermore, it may be expected that attempts to stipulate on jurisdiction in a manner that would restrict the effectiveness of an international court or erode its legitimacy would be resisted by the international court in question even in the absence of an explicit prohibition against such stipulations. The approach of the European Court of Human Rights (ECtHR) in the *Loizidou* case[11] and of Judge Lauterpacht in the *Norwegian Loans* and *Interhandel* cases,[12] both discussed in Part I of this book, illustrate such forms of resistance.

The upshot of this analysis is that the jurisdictional powers of international courts comprise two interlocked sets of jurisdictional authorization and conditions: (a) A foundational authorization, which is subject to jurisdictional conditions – all of which are derived from the relevant court's constitutive instruments and supplemented, at

8 ICSID Convention, art. 25(2)(b).

9 *Elettronica Sicula S.p.A.* (ELSI) (*USA* v. *Italy*), 1989 ICJ 15, 42.

10 ICC Statute, art. 120.

11 Loizidou v. Turkey, 1995 Eur. Ct. H.R. (ser. A) (No. 310)

12 *Interhandel* (*Switzerland* v. *US*), 1959 ICJ 6, 115 (Lauterpacht J., dissenting); *Certain Norwegian Loans* (*France* v. *Norway*), 1957 ICJ 9, 55 (Lauterpacht J., dissenting).

times, by general international law; and (b) a specific grant of jurisdictional authority invested in the relevant international court by those states or other international actors (including, sometimes, private parties) who are either the direct parties to the dispute or are closely related to the situation in hand (for instance, the state of nationality of a suspected international criminal or the state of nationality of a foreign investor). This specific grant of authority may be subject to another set of jurisdictional conditions. As a result, one can discuss the jurisdiction of an international court *in abstracto* – that is, what are the categories of cases it may hear on the basis of its foundational jurisdiction, and what jurisdictional conditions it is subject to, or *in concreto* – that is, did the combination of general and specific authorizations and conditions bring a particular dispute or situation under the purview of the Court's jurisdictional authority?

Unfortunately, a review of the international law literature and jurisprudence shows considerable confusion and inconsistency in employing the four principal categories I identified earlier in this book: foundational jurisdiction, general conditions, specific jurisdiction, and specific conditions. For example, in one of its 2004 judgments on *Use of Force (NATO)*, the ICJ addressed the question of its jurisdiction *ratione personae* over states as one of *access:*

> The Court can exercise its judicial function only in respect of those States which have access to it under Article 35 of the Statute. And only those States which have access to the Court can confer jurisdiction upon it.[13]

In my proposed terminology, however, 'access' is merely one element of foundational jurisdiction – foundational jurisdiction *ratione personae*. It corresponds to the authorization of the ICJ by the state parties to the Statute to hear cases submitted to it by certain states only (the state parties to the ICJ Statute and the state parties to jurisdiction-conferring treaties in force), subject to the foundational jurisdiction condition of consent. Indeed, in its 2007 judgment in *Application of the Genocide Convention* (*Bosnia* v. *Serbia*), the Court moved away from its earlier distinction between access and jurisdiction, and held instead held that questions of access might be seen as one element, of a preliminary nature, in establishing the Court's *ratione personae* jurisdiction:

[13] *Legality of Use of Force* (*Serbia and Montenegro* v. *Belgium*), 2004 ICJ 279, 299.

> [T]he question whether a State has the capacity under the Statute to be a party to proceedings before the Court . . . may be regarded as an issue prior to that of jurisdiction *ratione personae*, or as one constitutive element within the concept of jurisdiction *ratione personae*.[14]

The preliminary nature of foundational jurisdiction

While it may make little difference, in practice, whether any of the alternative terms – 'access', 'issue prior to jurisdiction *ratione personae*', or 'foundational jurisdiction *ratione personae*' – is being used, it is important to avoid the conceptual confusion over the relations between the different types of jurisdictional authorization and jurisdictional conditions, which the term 'access' may generate. First, we should understand questions of 'access', that is, regulation of the identity of international actors that can invest the Court with specific jurisdiction, as merely one element of foundational jurisdiction – that is, the overall powers *in abstracto* conferred upon the Court by the mandate providers. This is because one may identify other foundational jurisdiction authorizations and conditions, enjoying a similar preliminary status and limiting the capacity of international actors to confer jurisdiction upon international courts.

For example, the power of United Nations' organs and specialized agencies to request advisory opinions from the ICJ depends on satisfaction of the prior condition that they have been authorized to do so by the General Assembly (a condition, which may be regarded as a matter of 'access').[15] Still, the ability of such organs or agencies to request an advisory opinion is also limited by the foundational jurisdictional authorization that the request would deal with 'legal questions arising within the scope of their activities'.[16] This foundational jurisdictional requirement, which limits the Court's scope of jurisdiction *ratione materiae* in advisory proceedings, is also of a preliminary character in the sense that the Court is expected to address whether the request is *ultra vires* before addressing other questions of jurisdiction

[14] *Application of the Convention on the Prevention and Punishment of the Crime of Genocide* (*Bosnia and Herzegovina* v. *Serbia and Montenegro*), 2007 ICJ 43, 85.

[15] United Nations, Charter of the United Nations, San Francisco, 26 June 1945, in force 24 October 1945, art. 96(2), 1 UNTS XVI, available at: www.un.org/en/documents/charter/intro.shtml (hereinafter 'UN Charter').

[16] *Ibid., ibid.*

and admissibility.[17] Indeed, the ICJ has described the World Health Organization (WHO) request for an advisory opinion on the *Use by a State of Nuclear Weapons* as a 'fundamental defect'[18] – that is, failing to meet an 'essential condition', namely the *ratione materiae* limits set by article 96(2) of the United Nations Charter:

> Having arrived at the view that the request for an advisory opinion submitted by the WHO does not relate to a question which arises 'within the scope of [the] activities' of that Organization in accordance with Article 96, paragraph 2, of the Charter, the Court finds that an essential condition of founding its jurisdiction in the present case is absent and that it cannot, accordingly, give the opinion requested. Consequently, the Court is not called upon to examine the arguments which were laid before it with regard to the exercise of its discretionary power to give an opinion.[19]

One might have expected questions of foundational jurisdiction *ratione materiae* to arise only rarely for the ICJ given the very broad nature of its mandate in contentious cases and advisory proceedings initiated by the General Assembly and Security Council.[20] Still, the Court has grappled in a number of cases with the preliminary question of whether there is a 'legal dispute' between the parties to the proceedings,[21] construing in effect its foundational jurisdiction *ratione materiae* under article 36(1) of the ICJ Statute over 'all cases' or 'all matters' as limited to 'legal disputes' only (as explicitly provided for only in article 36(2) of the Statute).[22] In the same vein,

[17] *Legality of the Use by a State of Nuclear Weapons in Armed Conflict*, 1996 ICJ 66, 82.

[18] *Ibid.*, at 82. [19] *Ibid.*, at 84.

[20] ICJ Statute, art. 36 ('1. The jurisdiction of the Court comprises *all cases* which the parties refer to it and *all matters* specially provided for in the Charter of the United Nations or in treaties and conventions in force. 2. The states parties to the present Statute may at any time declare that they recognize as compulsory *ipso facto* and without special agreement, in relation to any other state accepting the same obligation, the jurisdiction of the Court in *all legal disputes* concerning ... (b) *any question of international law*') (emphasis added); UN Charter, art. 96(1) ('The General Assembly or the Security Council may request the International Court of Justice to give an advisory opinion on *any legal question* (emphasis added).

[21] See *South West Africa (Ethiopia* v. *South Africa)*, 1962 ICJ 319, 328 ('Before undertaking this task, however, the Court finds it necessary to decide a preliminary question relating to the existence of the dispute which is the subject of the Applications'). See also e.g. *Aegean Sea* (*Greece* v. *Turkey)*, 1978 ICJ 3, 13; *East Timor* (*Portugal* v. *Australia)*, 1995 ICJ 90, 99–100.

[22] See Christian Tomuschat, 'Article 36', in Andreas Zimmermann *et al.* (eds.), *The Statute of the International Court of Justice: A Commentary*, 2nd edn. (Oxford: Oxford University Press, 2012), pp. 643–644.

one may note that the Permanent Court of International Justice (PCIJ) has opined that disputes arising exclusively under municipal law might fall under certain circumstances within the scope of its subject-matter jurisdiction,[23] suggesting that the legal basis of the claims is another preliminary feature of foundational jurisdiction *ratione materiae* that the Court may examine on suitable occasions.[24]

To be sure, preliminary questions of foundational jurisdiction *ratione materiae* appear to be far more central to the operation of international courts invested with specialized subject-matter jurisdiction than to that of the ICJ. For example, there is a long line of ICSID cases dealing with the preliminary question of whether the dispute referred to ICSID arbitration arises from a 'foreign investment'.[25] Similar questions of foundational jurisdiction *ratione materiae* also arise sometime before human rights courts[26] and economic integration courts;[27] they may also arise in the future

[23] *Payment of Various Serbian Loans Issued in France* (*France* v. *Serbia*), 1929 PCIJ (Ser. A), No, 20/21, at 20 ('Article 38 of the Statute cannot be regarded as excluding the possibility of the Court's dealing with disputes which do not require the application of international law, seeing that the Statute itself expressly provides for this possibility').

[24] For the view that the ICJ may not follow the PCIJ on this foundational jurisdiction matter, see Alain Pellet, 'Article 38', in *The Statute of the International Court of Justice,* note 22, pp. 658–659, 731, 780.

[25] See e.g. *Aguas del Tunari, S.A.* v. *Bolivia,* ICSID Case No. ARB/02/3, Decision on Jurisdiction of 21 October 2005, at para 278 ('This Tribunal is established pursuant to the ICSID Convention and its jurisdiction is limited by the ICSID Convention, as defined in Article 25. This Tribunal must therefore evaluate whether the dispute presented to it under the BIT passes through the jurisdictional keyhole defined by Article 25 of the ICSID Convention'); *Fedax NV* v. *Venezuela,* Decision on Jurisdiction of 11 July 1997, ICSID Case No. ARB/96/3, at para 21 ('The Tribunal shall first examine the meaning of the term "investment" under Article 25(1) of the Convention').

[26] See e.g. *Malarde* v. *France,* ECtHR Decision on Admissibility of 5 September 2000, at para 2; *X and Y* v. *Germany,* App. No, 7407/76 Eur. HR Com'n Decision on Admissibility of 13 May 1976, 5 DR 161; *Chacha* v. *Tanzania,* App. No. 003/2012, African Court of Human and Peoples' Rights Ruling of 28 March 2014, at paras 112–124.

[27] See e.g. *Asia Motor France SA* v. *Commission,* 1996 ECR II-961, at para 32 ('the Community courts have no jurisdiction to give a ruling, at an applicant's initiative, on the compatibility of natural or legal persons' conduct with the provisions of the Treaty'); Laudo No 01/2012 (Award 1/2012), Tribunal Permanente de Revisión del Mercosur, of 21 July 2012, paras 29–43.

before the United National Convention on the Law of Sea (UNCLOS) dispute settlement bodies[28] and the ICC.[29]

For some international courts, other foundational jurisdiction aspects hold a prominent preliminary character. For instance, the International Criminal Tribunal for Rwanda (ICTR) needed to ensure that crimes prosecuted before it fell within the scope of its jurisdiction *ratione temporis* (crimes committed in 1994)[30] and similar issues may arise before the ICC in future.[31] In addition, international human rights courts have dealt in several high-profile cases with foundational jurisdiction *ratione loci* issues.[32]

In all of these cases, not only those involving questions of 'access', international courts must satisfy themselves that they potentially have the legal power to adjudicate the dispute – that is, that they have been entrusted with proper foundational jurisdiction. Although international courts normally retain discretion on the order in which different questions of jurisdiction, admissibility and merits are discussed, it often makes sense to deal with questions relating to foundational jurisdiction – that is to say, whether the referred case falls within the outer limits of the court's legal powers – prior to reviewing the existence and applicability of specific authorizations, specific conditions and admissibility criteria. This is because it is usually easier to determine questions of legal capacity (jurisdiction) than questions relating to whether legal capacity should be exercised (admissibility), and because the terms of the specific jurisdictional authorizations and conditions invested in an international court by the disputing

[28] For example, under art. 21 of the UNCLOS, Annex VI – Statute of the International Tribunal for the Law of the Sea (ITLOS) (hereinafter 'ITLOS Statute'), the tribunal has jurisdiction over 'all disputes and all applications submitted to it in accordance with this Convention and all matters specifically provided for in any other agreement which confers jurisdiction on the Tribunal'.

[29] E.g., under art. 8bis(1) of the ICC Statute, the Court would have jurisdiction over an act of aggression only if it 'by its character, gravity and scale, constitutes a manifest violation of the Charter of the United Nations'.

[30] Statute of the International Criminal Tribunal for Rwanda, Security Council, 8 November 1994, art. 1, Resolution 955 (1994), UN Doc. S/RES/955. See also *Prosecutor* v. *Nahimana,* Case No. ICTR-99–52-A, Appeals Chamber Judgment of 28 November 2007, at para 318.

[31] ICC Statute, art. 11. For a discussion of the Court's jurisdiction *ratione temporis,* see Alexander Willis, 'Old Crimes, New States and the Temporal Jurisdiction of the International Criminal Court' (2014) 12 JICJ 407.

[32] See e.g. *Bankovic* v. *Belgium,* App. No. 52207/99, ECtHR decision of 12 December 2001; HRC, *Lopez Burgos* v. *Uruguay,* Communication No. R.12/52, paras 12.1–12.3, U.N. Doc. Supp. No. 40 (A/36/40) at 176 (1981).

parties are regulated by the terms of its foundational jurisdiction and derive their legal effect vis-à-vis the Court from these terms.

Hierarchical relations between jurisdictional bases

The second aspect, which the use of the term 'access' by the ICJ in *Use of Force (NATO)* does not fully capture, is the hierarchical relationship holding between foundational and specific jurisdiction. Such a hierarchical relationship largely reflects the legal relations holding between the international court's mandate providers and the specific disputing parties attempting to seize it.

The mandate providers, who typically comprise the state parties to the instrument or international organization establishing an international court, can create rights and obligations governing the legal relations among themselves and their relations to the new court. For example, all parties to the Court's statute may have to provide it with funding[33] and enforce its judgments,[34] and all of them may participate in the election of judges[35] and can use its dispute resolution services under certain conditions.[36] The mandate providers can also create rights and obligations for third parties who may wish to utilize the international court they created, including states not parties to its constitutive instruments, private parties and international organizations.[37] In such cases, consent by a third party to participate in judicial proceedings under the terms provided in the constitutive instruments (and actual participation in judicial proceedings can be regarded as a form of tacit consent to such terms) implies an acceptance of the conditions or obligations attendant to the third-party rights created by the mandate providers.[38]

Since the constitutive instruments promulgated by the mandate providers envision the conclusion of specific jurisdiction instruments (e.g. in the form of *compromis* or acceptance of optional clause declarations) or other specific jurisdiction stipulations (e.g. in the form of reservations or the specific terms of the application to adjudication), and purport to regulate their contents, one may regard the explicit or implicit acceptance of the terms of the constitutive instruments, including their foundational jurisdiction provisions, by the disputing

[33] See e.g. ICC Statute, art. 115. [34] See e.g. ICSID Convention, art. 54.
[35] See e.g. ACHR, art. 53. [36] See e.g. DSU, art. 6. [37] See e.g. ECHR, art. 34.
[38] VCLT, art. 36.

parties as acceptance of the hierarchical superiority of foundational jurisdiction over specific jurisdiction. In the same vein, the international court established by the mandate providers has been sometimes instructed in its constitutive instrument to evaluate subsequent attempts by disputing parties to invoke its jurisdiction based on its foundational jurisdiction criteria.[39] This too signifies a hierarchical configuration of the relations between foundational and specific jurisdiction.

Some of the *dicta* employed by the ICJ in *Use of Force (NATO)* on the relationship between questions of *access* (foundational jurisdiction) and *consent-based* jurisdiction (specific jurisdiction) treat the terms of its foundational jurisdiction as overriding any inconsistent terms defining the specific jurisdiction over the case before it, though it stops short of explicitly finding a hierarchical relationship between the two types of jurisdiction:

> [A] distinction has to be made between a question of jurisdiction that relates to the consent of a party and the question of the right of a party to appear before the Court under the requirements of the Statute, which is not a matter of consent. The question is whether as a matter of law Serbia and Montenegro was entitled to seise the Court as a party to the Statute at the time when it instituted proceedings in these cases. Since that question is independent of the views or wishes of the Parties, even if they were now to have arrived at a shared view on the point, the Court would not have to accept that view as necessarily the correct one. The function of the Court to enquire into the matter and reach its own conclusion is thus mandatory upon the Court irrespective of the consent of the parties and is in no way incompatible with the principle that the jurisdiction of the Court depends on consent.[40]

According to the Court, it must independently verify the existence of its foundational and specific jurisdiction, and the existence of the latter does not necessarily imply the existence of the former. While this is no doubt true, the more profound point – that specific jurisdiction derives from foundational jurisdiction and is governed by its terms – has not been explicitly acknowledged by the Court.

Indeed, a key aspect of the relationship between the two types of jurisdiction is that specific jurisdiction cannot deviate from the

[39] See e.g. ICC Statute, art. 53 (the Court may review decision by a Prosecutor not to prosecute a case referred to it by a State party or the Security Council by reason of failure to meet the Statute's jurisdiction and admissibility standards).

[40] *Legality of Use of Force* (*Serbia and Montenegro* v. *Belgium*), 2004 ICJ 279, at 295.

foundational jurisdiction framework. This is supported by the prohibition found in the Vienna Convention on the Law of Treaties against unilaterally creating third-party obligations,[41] which implies that disputing parties participating in adjudication before an international court cannot create new obligations for the mandate providers without the latter's express consent. Were the disputing parties able to extend the jurisdiction of an international court beyond the scope originally contemplated by the mandate providers, such an extension might have placed new burdens on the mandate providers who may need to fund the new unforeseen litigation, and might have reduced their expected returns from the Court, since it would now lack the time and resources to engage in the types of adjudication foreseen by the mandate providers. Analogous concerns may arise, however, also in relation to inefficient *intra vires* utilization of an international court's jurisdictional powers. For example, some of the criticisms directed against the policy by the International Criminal Tribunal for Yugoslavia (ICTY) Prosecutor in the first years of the Tribunal to indict low-level perpetrators, invoked concerns that litigating such cases would require the mandate providers to fund the adjudication of cases very different from the ones they have expected, and would necessarily detract from the resources available to adjudicate more serious cases.[42]

[41] VCLT, art. 35.

[42] See ICTY Press Release CC/PIO/003E, The Judges of the Tribunal for the former Yugoslavia express their concern regarding the substance of their programme of judicial work for 1995, 1 February 1995:

> Due to the gravity and historic dimension of that mission, the Judges are anxious that a programme of indictments should effectively meet the expectations of the Security Council and of the world community at large. The Prosecutor was informed of the concern of the Judges, and he indicated that he shares that concern. He undertook to apply the resources that have now been made available by the United Nations and by those Member States which have generously contributed to the Trust Fund, in order to issue appropriate indictments at the earliest possible time.

See Sarah Williams, 'The Completion Strategy of the ICTY and the ICTR', in Michael Bohlander (ed.) *International Criminal Justice: A Critical Analysis of Institutions and Procedures* (London: Cameron May, 2007), pp. 153, 156. See also S.C. Res 1329 (2000), UN Doc. S/RES/1329 (2000) ('Taking note of the position expressed by the International Tribunals that civilian, military and paramilitary leaders should be tried before them in preference to minor actors.'); Statement by the president of the Security Council, 23 July 2002, UN Doc. S/PRST/2002/21 ('the ICTY should concentrate its work on the prosecution and trial of the civilian, military and paramilitary leaders

In the same vein, the disputing parties should not be able to impose new obligations on the international court, which they attempt to seize. This is because the court itself constitutes another third party over whose structure and procedures the disputing parties are not entitled to exercise broad legal control, since it has been created and is being maintained by a broader constituency of states or international organizations. Furthermore, one might argue that the disputing parties should not be in a position to extend the jurisdiction of an international court beyond the scope originally contemplated by the mandate providers, because such an expansion might compromise the Court's ability to fulfil its original mandate (i. e. effectiveness)[43] and to retain broad acceptance of its authority by its constituencies (i.e. legitimacy).[44] It may also create practical difficulties for the Court seized, in those cases where the new grounds of specific jurisdiction entrusted to it entail procedural consequences not envisioned in its constitutive instruments.

Jurisdictional 'hijacking'

All the previous legal and policy considerations support treating foundational jurisdiction as hierarchically superior to specific jurisdiction. Without it, the disputing parties would be able to 'hijack' the jurisdiction of international courts, instruct them to perform judicial tasks

suspected of being responsible for serious violations of international humanitarian law committed in the territory of the former Yugoslavia since 1991, rather than on minor actors').

[43] *Cf.* Letter by African civil society organizations and international organizations to Justice Ministers and Attorneys General of African states parties to the International Criminal Court, 3 May 2012, www.hrw.org/sites/default/files/related_material/Letter_on_African_Court_May_2012.pdf:

> The expansion of the African Court's jurisdiction risks undermining progress in the development of Africa's human rights system. The merger between the existing African Court on Human and Peoples' Rights and the African Court of Justice could already dilute the work of the former. Adding a third [international criminal law] mandate to the African Court will further drain away resources needed to shore up the African Court's human rights mandate.

[44] See e.g. Lawrence R Helfer and Karen J Alter, 'Legitimacy and Lawmaking: A Tale of Three International Courts' (2013) 14 *Theoretical Inquiries in Law* 478, 489 ('these examples suggest that certain types of expansive [International Court] lawmaking – in particular, the use of aggressively teleological interpretive methods or the expansion of subject matter competencies – sometimes trigger legitimacy challenges').

unrelated to their mission and thereby compromise the rights and interests of the mandate providers and the international courts themselves. It is for such reasons that international courts are expected to examine *proprio motu* the suitability of cases referred to them by the disputing parties with their foundational jurisdiction framework.[45]

An example of the serious difficulties created by a situation bordering on jurisdictional 'hijacking', involving a court procedure hardly envisioned by the mandate providers, can be found in the recent ICJ Advisory Opinion on *ILOAT/IFAD*. The case was initiated by a request submitted to the Court by the International Fund for Agricultural Development (IFAD) to review an administrative tribunal ruling issued against it in a case brought by one of its employees. The Court strongly criticized a key aspect of the review process – the inequality in the right of access to the Court of the employing IGO and the employee – that the Court deemed to run contrary to the principle of equality of the parties:

> [T]he Court is unable to see any such justification for the provision for review of the Tribunal's decisions which favours the employer to the disadvantage of the staff member.[46]

Still, despite the palpable unease it felt about adjudicating the IFAD request, the Court ultimately held that the flaws in the process were not sufficiently grave to justify declining jurisdiction over the case:

[45] See *Application of the Convention on the Prevention and Punishment of the Crime of Genocide* (*Bosnia and Herzegovina* v. *Serbia and Montenegro*), 2007 ICJ 43, at 94:

> the question whether a state may properly come before the Court, on the basis of the provisions of the Statute, whether it be classified as a matter of capacity to be a party to the proceedings or as an aspect of jurisdiction *ratione personae*, is a matter which precedes that of jurisdiction *ratione materiae* . . . The question is in fact one which the Court is bound to raise and examine, if necessary, ex officio.

Note the confusion between the nature of jurisdictional title (*foundational* v. *specific*) and the dimension of jurisdictional authorization (*ratione personae* v. *ratione materiae*). See also Gerald Fitzmaurice, 'The Law and Procedure of the International Court of Justice, 1951–4: Questions of Jurisdiction, Competence and Procedure' (1958) 34 Brit. Y.B. Int'l L., 28–29. *Cf. Minority Schools in Upper Silesia* (*Germany* v. *Poland*), 1928 PCIJ (Ser. A), No. 12, at 23 (noting that for national courts, whose jurisdiction is determined within a hierarchical system, 'the raising of an objection by one Party merely draws the attention of the Court to an objection to the jurisdiction which it must *ex officio* consider').

[46] *Judgment No. 2867 of the Administrative Tribunal of the International Labour Organization upon a Complaint Filed against the International Fund for Agricultural Development*, 2012 ICJ 10, 27.

Notwithstanding these difficulties, the Court concludes that, by the end of the process, it does have the information it requires to decide on the questions submitted ... and that, in essence, the principle of equality in the proceedings before the Court, required by its inherent judicial character and by the good administration of justice, has been met.[47]

At a more general level, we may regard the IFAD request as a successful attempt to 'hijack' the jurisdiction of the ICJ for a mode of operation not necessarily envisioned by the mandate providers – the use of the ICJ as an appellate labour court.[48] Such potential misuse of the Court not only diverts scarce judicial resources from the Court's more central missions (such as contributing to international peace and security), but also puts the Court's procedures under significant pressure, since they were not geared to accommodate disputes between individuals and intergovernmental organizations (IGOs).[49] The Court may have had no choice but to accept jurisdiction over the case, since the request did formally fall within the purview of article 96(2) of the United Nations Charter, and indeed on previous occasions it had accepted jurisdiction over IGO requests to review administrative tribunal rulings.[50] However, I am not persuaded of the wisdom of the Court's decision to refrain from invoking its discretionary powers to declare the case as inadmissible. Given the serious shortcomings of the legal procedure presented by the case, the concerns about misuse of the judicial process, the negative signal that was sent to the Court by the mandate providers,

[47] *Ibid.*, at 30.

[48] Interestingly enough, the UN General Assembly did allow between 1955 and 1995 the Court to be utilized for review of the United Nations Administrative Tribunal rulings through a process that provided access to both the IGO and its employee. The process was ultimately abandoned in 1995. UN General Assembly Resolution 50/54, 11 December 1995, UN Doc. A/RES/50/54 (1996).

[49] The IFAD proceedings did not even have the benefit of the corrective mechanism introduced by the now defunct UN Committee on Applications for Review. See Paul Szasz, 'Adjudicating Staff Challenges to Legislative Decisions of International Organizations', in Gerhard Hafner *et al.* (eds.), *Lieber Amicorum Professor Ignaz Seidl-Hohenveldern* (The Hague: Kluwer Law International, 1998), p. 715.

[50] *Judgments of the Administrative Tribunal of the ILO upon Complaints Made against Unesco*, 1956 ICJ 77; *Application for Review of Judgment No. 158 of the United Nations Administrative Tribunal*, 1973 ICJ 166; *Application for Review of Judgment No. 273 of the United Nations Administrative Tribunal*, 1982 ICJ 325; *Application for Review of Judgment No. 333 of the United Nations Administrative Tribunal*, 1987 ICJ 18.

who in 1995 revoked the parallel the United Nations Administrative Tribunal review process, and the increasing pressures on the Court's time exacted by the growing case load, the grounds for declining jurisdiction over the case were in my eyes sufficiently compelling.

Be this as it may, it is clear that in cases of jurisdictional 'hijacking' deviating from the Court's foundational jurisdiction, the Court should defend its general jurisdictional framework, notwithstanding any relevant policy considerations. This is because deviations from the terms of foundational jurisdiction that were laid down by the mandate providers are, as a rule, non-curable (unless the mandate providers themselves consent to it).[51] In this respect, deviations from foundational jurisdiction are different from deviations from specific jurisdiction in that the disputing parties may cure jurisdictional problems relating to the terms of the latter by agreeing to deviate therefrom (though international courts may be authorized to decide whether or not to accept the admissibility of such 'cured' deviations). Thus, for example, in the WHO *Legality of the Use by a State of Nuclear Weapons* advisory opinion, once the Court held that the WHO request deviated from the terms of the Courts' foundational jurisdiction *ratione materiae*, it had no choice but to reject the request.[52]

By contrast, the doctrine of *forum prorogatum* stipulates that a unilateral attempt to seize the jurisdiction of the ICJ without the consent of the respondent party may succeed if the latter party appears before the Court without challenging its jurisdiction.[53] Put differently, lack of consent to a specific application to the ICJ constitutes a deviation from the terms of the Court's specific jurisdiction *ratione personae*, which may be cured by the implicit consent to jurisdiction of the participating respondent party (unless the Court finds another reason to deem the case inadmissible).[54]

[51] For a discussion of the curability of consent-based jurisdictional terms, see Chittharanjan F Amerasinghe, *Jurisdiction of International Tribunals* (The Hague: Kluwer Law International, 2003), p. 198.

[52] *Legality of the Use by a State of Nuclear Weapons in Armed Conflict*, 1996 ICJ 66, at 73 ('The Court can however only exercise this discretionary power if it has first established that it has jurisdiction in the case in question; if the Court lacks jurisdiction, the question of exercising its discretionary power does not arise').

[53] See *Corfu Channel* (*UK* v. *Albania*) 1948 ICJ 15, 27; Shabtai Rosenne, 'The Forum Prorogatum in the International Court of Justice', (1953) 6 Revue hellénique de droit international 1.

[54] Another, more difficult, example of a curable flaw in specific jurisdiction may be found in the *Wall* case, where it was claimed before the Court that in presenting a

If I am right in concluding that the terms of foundational jurisdiction trump the terms of specific jurisdiction – that is, that any grant of authority an international court by the disputing parties and the jurisdictional conditions that attach thereto must remain within the contours of the authority conferred upon the Court by its mandate providers and the jurisdictional conditions they introduced – then we may question the legal soundness of the decision reached by the ICJ in the *Application of the Genocide Convention* (*Bosnia* v. *Serbia*) case on the *res judicata* effect of its 1996 judgment on preliminary objections.[55] In its 2007 judgment on the merits of the case, the Court rejected Serbia's argument that the principle of *res judicata* cannot allow it to operate *ultra vires* (i.e. issue a judgment against a non-state party), and held that the 1996 judgment settled the question of access to the Court (or, in our terminology, foundational jurisdictional) and that it cannot be reopened due to the finality of judgments principle. Putting aside some of the thorny doctrinal questions, which the 2007 judgment raises – in particular, whether judgments on preliminary objections generate a *res judicata* effect in a subsequent stage of the same proceedings,[56] whether new 'legal

request for an advisory opinion on a matter which was pending before the Security Council, the General Assembly had breached article 12(1) of the Charter, which regulated the division of labour between the two principal organs. Put differently, it was alleged that whereas the application fell within the terms of the Court's foundational jurisdiction, the applying organ acted *ultra vires* with respect to another set of international norms that regulated its conduct, and thus did not validly refer the matter to the Court in a manner that would invest it with specific jurisdiction over the specific request. The Court's response was that art. 12(1) was, in practice, construed very flexibly and that, as a result, no breach of the Charter had occurred. This reasoning may be tantamount to viewing UN practice as a cure to a specific jurisdictional flaw. *Legal Consequences of the Construction of a Wall in the Occupied Palestinian Territory*, 2004 ICJ 136, 150:

> The Court considers that the accepted practice of the General Assembly, as it has evolved, is consistent with article 12, paragraph 1, of the Charter. The Court is accordingly of the view that the General Assembly, in adopting resolution ES-10114, seeking an advisory opinion from the Court, did not contravene the provisions of Article 12, paragraph 1 of the Charter. The Court concludes that by submitting that request the General Assembly did not exceed its competence.

55 *Application of the Convention on the Prevention and Punishment of the Crime of Genocide* (*Bosnia and Herzegovina* v. *Serbia and Montenegro*), 2007 ICJ 43, at 101–102.

56 For a discussion, see Stephen Wittich, 'Permissible Derogation from Mandatory Rules? The Problem of Party Status in the Genocide Case' (2007) 18 *EJIL* 591, 600–604. Arguably, the holding in *Application of the Genocide Convention* deviates from the judgment in the *South West Africa* case. *South West Africa* (*Ethiopia* v. *South Africa*), 1966 ICJ 6, 36–37 (ICJ reserving judgment on whether judgments on

facts' can lead to judgment revision,[57] and whether the principle of *res judicata* overrides the principle of *ultra vires*[58] – one is left with the no less difficult question of the compatibility of the judgment with the basic structure of the jurisdiction of the international court. Since none of the parties to the 1996 judgment challenged the foundational jurisdiction *ratione personae* of the Court,[59] their acquiescence had in actuality the same effect as a specific agreement by the adjudicating parties to stipulate on the Court's foundational jurisdiction. The ICJ could, of course, have raised the issue of foundational jurisdiction *proprio motu* in its 1996 judgment, but it did not do so. Under these circumstances, it is hard for me to see how the case can be regarded as 'settled' for *res judicata* purposes.[60] Furthermore, given the fundamental nature of foundational jurisdiction, and its impact on the rights and interest of third parties (i.e. the mandate providers), one would expect international courts to proceed cautiously in applying a rule of procedure (*res judicata*) to arrogate to themselves legal powers which they were not intended to possess. The aforementioned questions surrounding the doctrinal propriety of the application of *res judicata* in the 2007 judgment do not appear to meet such a standard of judicial caution. As a result, I find the joint

preliminary objections create a *res judicata* effect, and, in effect, reversing in 1962 judgment).

57 For a discussion, see Wittich, 'Permissible Derogation from Mandatory Rules?', at 596–595 (discussing the 2003 decision in which the ICJ refused to revise its 1996 judgment on preliminary objections).

58 *Cf.* H. William R Wade and Christopher Forsyth, *Administrative Law*, 11th edn. (New York: Oxford University Press, 2014), p. 205 ('No question of res judicata can derogate from the rules that a determination that is ultra vires may always be challenged in the High Court and that no tribunal can give itself jurisdiction which it does not possess'); Xavier Groussot and Timo Minssen, 'Res Judicata in the Court of Justice Case-Law: Balancing Legal Certainty with Legality?' (2007) *European Constitutional Law Review* 385, 414–415 ('*res judicata*, an emanation of the principle of legal certainty, is not absolute and must carefully be balanced with Community legality').

59 *Application of the Convention on the Prevention and Punishment of the Crime of Genocide* (*Bosnia and Herzegovina* v. *Serbia and Montenegro*), 2007 ICJ 43, at 87 ('Neither of the parties raised the matter before the Court').

60 See Bin Cheng, *General Principles of Law as Applied by International Courts and Tribunals* (Cambridge: Cambridge University Press, 1953), p. 337 (the *res judicata* principle means that rights, questions and facts distinctly put in issue and directly determined by a competent court cannot be disputed). None of the three elements noted by Cheng – distinct discussion, direct determination and competence – appears to have been clearly met by the 1996 judgment with relation to foundational jurisdiction *ratione personae*.

dissent issued by judges Rajeev, Shi and Koroma, arguing for a contextualized application of the principle of *res judicata* to those specific aspects of jurisdiction actually determined by the Court, far more persuasive on this point than the approach of the Court's majority.[61]

Hierarchy between foundational and specific jurisdiction in other courts

Of course, concerns about incidents of jurisdictional 'hijacking' that are incompatible with the hierarchical relations holding between foundational and specific jurisdiction are not unique to the ICJ. For instance, ICSID arbitral tribunals have held that the parties cannot agree to define an 'investment' in terms broader than that provided in article 25 of the ICSID Convention.[62] Here too, the terms of foundational jurisdiction delimit the space available for the disputing parties to agree upon the specific terms of adjudication. Moreover, ICSID tribunals have also on occasion been required to address the implications of changes in private ownership, which appeared to remove an investor involved in ICSID arbitration from the scope of foundational jurisdiction *ratione personae* under the ICSID Convention, but which took place after the jurisdiction of the ICSID had already been established. Although the language used by some ICSID tribunals reflects unease about exercising

[61] *Application of the Convention on the Prevention and Punishment of the Crime of Genocide* (*Bosnia and Herzegovina* v. *Serbia and Montenegro*), 2007 ICJ 43, at 269–270 (dissenting opinion of judges Ranjeva, Shi and Koroma) ('the scope and effect of res judicata for purposes of jurisdiction *ratione personae* must be determined by reference to the law of the case itself ... It is thus obvious that not all of the elements of jurisdiction *ratione personae* were actually placed before and decided by the Court in its 1996 Judgment and, accordingly, that the *res judicata* effect of that judgment for this issue is unsustainable to say the least').

[62] See e.g. *Joy Mining Machinery Ltd.* v. *Egypt*, ICSID Case No. ARB/03/11, at para 50 ('The parties to a dispute cannot by contract or treaty define as investment, for the purpose of ICSID jurisdiction, something which does not satisfy the objective requirements of Article 25 of the Convention. Otherwise Article 25 and its reliance on the concept of investment, even if not specifically defined, would be turned into a meaningless provision'); *Malaysian Historical Savors SDN, BHD* v. *Malaysia*, ICSID Case No. ARB/05/10, Award on Jurisdiction of 17 May 2007, at para 55 ('a finding that the Contract satisfied the definition of "investment" under the BIT would not be sufficient for this Tribunal to assume jurisdiction, if the Contract failed to satisfy the objective criterion of an "investment" within the meaning of Article 25').

jurisdiction over investors that the ICSID Convention was not designed to protect (e.g. investments now owned by host-state natural or legal persons), they tended to embrace the rule that jurisdiction should be established at a critical date (the date in which consent to ICSID jurisdiction was afforded), and that subsequent factual changes should not affect this determination.[63]

As noted earlier, when discussing deviations from foundational jurisdiction a distinction should be made between situations of authorized and unauthorized jurisdictional deviations. Whereas the parties to a dispute cannot deviate at will from the foundational jurisdiction framework governing the operations of an international court, there is nothing to bar them from investing an international court with new jurisdictional powers, if the constitutive instruments so permit.[64] Such permissions to deviate are sometimes found in the constitutive instruments of international courts other than the ICJ. For example, article 272 of the Treaty on the Functioning of the European Union invests the Court of Justice of the European Union with jurisdiction to arbitrate disputes pursuant to contracts concluded by the EU,[65] and article 21 of the International Tribunal for the Law of the Sea (ITLOS) Statute confers on the Tribunal jurisdiction under 'any other agreement which confers jurisdiction on the Tribunal'.[66]

At times, international courts may be confronted with the question whether they may adjudicate a matter not explicitly covered by the terms of foundational jurisdiction articulated by the mandate providers. For instance, at the time of writing, ITLOS is considering a challenge to its power to issue advisory opinions in matters falling outside the jurisdiction of the Sea-Bed Chamber (which UNCLOS explicitly authorizes to receive advisory opinions).[67] Although the

63 Christoph H Schreuer, *The ICSID Convention: A Commentary*, 2nd edn. (Cambridge: Cambridge University Press, 2009), pp. 330–334.

64 See e.g. the 1992 *Morgan* case before the World Bank Administrative Tribunal (WBAT) (not published), where the tribunal declined to hear the case for lack of jurisdiction *ratione personae* under its Statute notwithstanding the agreement of the parties to invest it with such. The case was discussed in Amerasinghe, *Jurisdiction of International Tribunals*, pp. 88–89.

65 TFEU, art. 272.

66 ITLOS Statute, art. 21. Such an agreement must, however, be related to the purposes of UNCLOS. See UNCLOS, art. 288(2).

67 UNCLOS, art. 191. Shortly after this book went to print, ITLOS issued its decision on the matter (Case No. 21, *Request for an Advisory Opinion submitted by the Sub-Regional Fisheries Commission (SRFC)*, ITLOS Advisory Opinion of 2 April 2015), in which it uphold its authority to issue advisory opinions.

Rules set by the Tribunal itself allow for requests of advisory opinions,[68] a number of member states have argued that the procedure is *ultra vires.*[69] Other member states have argued that the silence of UNCLOS on the matter should not be considered as a bar to the exercise of advisory jurisdiction by the Tribunal.[70] Ultimately, the controversy over the power of ITLOS to introduce a new advisory procedure may revolve around the question whether the language of UNCLOS and the ITLOS Statute[71] implicitly authorizes the Tribunal to deviate from the foundational jurisdictional terms of United Nations Convention on the Law of the Sea (UNCLOS) and introduce a new procedure not explicitly sanctioned by the mandate providers.

68 Rules of the International Tribunal for the Law of the Sea, 28 October 1997, art. 138, ITLOS Doc. ITLOS/8 (as amended).

69 Case No. 21, *Request for an Advisory Opinion submitted by the Sub-Regional Fisheries Commission (SRFC),* written statement made on behalf of the UK government, 28 November 2013, at para 35; Case No. 21, *Request for an Advisory Opinion submitted by the Sub-Regional Fisheries Commission (SRFC),* written statement made on behalf of Australia, 28 November 2013, at para 39.

70 See e.g. Case No. 21, *Request for an Advisory Opinion submitted by the Sub-Regional Fisheries Commission (SRFC),* written statement made on behalf of Japan, 29 November 2013, at para 6; Case No. 21, *Request for an Advisory Opinion submitted by the Sub-Regional Fisheries Commission (SRFC),* written statement made on behalf of New Zealand, 27 November 2013, at para 10.

71 In particular, UNCLOS, Annex VI, art. 21 ('The jurisdiction of the Tribunal comprises all disputes and all applications submitted to it in accordance with this Convention and all matters specifically provided for in any other agreement which confers jurisdiction on the Tribunal').

7

Distinguishing jurisdiction from substantive law

Intertwined nature of jurisdictional and substantive questions

Before proceeding to a discussion of the main categories of jurisdictional authorizations and conditions governing the work of international courts, it may be useful to distinguish between the treatment of questions of jurisdiction and question of substantive law. At first glance, this is a rather straightforward distinction: Questions of jurisdiction revolve around the power to adjudicate a dispute, whereas substantive law questions revolve around the resolution of the pending dispute through identification of the relevant legal norms and their application to the facts of the case. The two questions also seem to belong to different stages of the adjudicative procedure: Substantive questions can only be reached after jurisdiction had already been established. Still, in the real world of international adjudication the two sets of issues are not always neatly distinguishable – neither analytically nor procedurally.

First, questions of jurisdiction and questions belonging to the merits of the case may rest on a common factual or legal basis. For example, a challenge against the legal validity of a bilateral investment treaty (BIT) containing both a compromissory clause and substantive rights and obligations, may implicate both jurisdictional questions and the merits of the case.[1] In the same vein, the question of whether or not a state exercises effective control over an area

[1] See e.g. *CSOB* v. *Slovakia*, ICSID Case No. ARB/97/4, Decision on Jurisdiction of 24 May 1999, at paras 37–43; *Eureko BV* v. *Slovakia*, PCA Case No. 2008–13, Award on Jurisdiction, Arbitrability and Suspension of 26 October 2010, at para 63 *et seq.*

located outside its territory may raise for international human rights courts questions of jurisdiction *ratione loci*, but it may also affect the analysis of the substantive obligations of the relevant state vis-à-vis residents under international human rights law.[2]

Second, if the applicant party to the proceedings had failed to show that the respondent party has assumed a relevant legal obligation towards it or that the respondent party has engaged in an act or omission that would bring the dispute within the scope of legal norms which the relevant international court is authorized to apply, then one could arguably claim that the case should not have been brought to the said court to begin with. This is because the scope of the court's *ratione materiae* authority is often defined by way of allusion to disputes over certain legal questions, such as the interpretation and application of a specific convention,[3] or questions falling under specific legal categories such as investment disputes[4] or human rights instruments.[5] A failure to establish a relationship between the claims made by the applicant party and the court's jurisdiction *ratione materiae* implies simultaneously that the court is not authorized to hear the claims and that the applicant party's substantive claims ought to be rejected. As a result, some international courts, as well as some international bodies with quasi-adjudicative powers such as the United Nations Human Rights Committee, regard the jurisdictional phase of the proceedings as containing a preliminary review of the substance of the applicant party's legal claims and the evidence supporting them.[6] If the applicant party fails to show a *prima facie* case on the merits, then the application would be dismissed as 'incompatible with the provisions of the Convention', 'manifestly ill-founded' or 'unsubstantiated'.[7] One can understand

[2] See e.g. *Loizidou* v. *Turkey*, 1995 Eur. Ct. H.R. (ser. A) (No. 310), at para 62; *Ilascu* v. *Moldova and Russia*, ECtHR judgment of 8 July 2004, at paras. 392–394.

[3] See e.g. Genocide Convention, art. 9; Optional Protocol to the Vienna Convention on Diplomatic Relations concerning the Compulsory Settlement of Disputes, 18 April 1961, in force 24 April 1961, art. I, 596 UNTS 261.

[4] ICSID Convention, art. 25.

[5] Protocol to the African Charter on Human and Peoples' Rights on the Establishment of an African Court on Human and Peoples' Rights, 10 June 1998, art. 3, www.achpr.org/instruments/court-establishment/; ACHR, art. 64.

[6] See Chittharanjan F Amerasinghe, *Jurisdiction of International Tribunals* (The Hague: Kluwer Law International, 2003), pp. 767–770.

[7] See ECHR, art. 35(3)(a); 'Optional Protocol to the International Covenant on Civil and Political Rights', 16 December 1966, in force 23 March 1976, art. 3, 999 UNTS 302 (hereinafter 'Optional Protocol to the ICCPR'); Human Rights

this process of preliminary review of substance in two different ways, as follows: (a) As an investigation of jurisdiction: before fully adjudicating the case, international courts must establish that the claims are plausibly related to their jurisdiction *ratione materiae* and thus come with their scope of authority; (b) as a matter of admissibility: international courts can be authorized for reasons of judicial economy to summarily dismiss hopeless claims which clearly have no chance of prevailing on their merits.[8]

The willingness of some international courts to examine, in a preliminary manner, the substance of the parties' factual and legal claims, underscores the observation that the distinction between questions of jurisdiction (and admissibility) and questions belonging to the merits is not always sharp in nature. The obfuscation of this distinction is further exacerbated by the fact that, as a practical matter, international courts often have considerable discretion in managing the order of the proceedings before them for a variety of reasons, including procedural economy.[9] They may decide, for instance, to join questions of jurisdiction to the merits,[10] or to dispose of the dispute on substantive grounds at the jurisdictional stage of the proceedings.[11]

The ICJ's approach to distinguishing jurisdiction from substance

A few examples may illustrate some of the specific difficulties associated with distinguishing between jurisdictional and substantive

Committee, Rule of Procedure (as amended on 11 January 2012), Rule 96(b), UN Doc. CCPR/C.3/Rev.10 (2012).

8 See Caroline Evans, *Freedom of Religion under the European Convention of Human Rights* (Oxford: Oxford University Press, 2001), p. 9.

9 See e.g. Christoph H Schreuer, *The ICSID Convention: A Commentary*, 2nd edn. (Cambridge: Cambridge University Press, 2009), p. 537.

10 See e.g. ICJ Rules of Court, Rule 79(9), 14 April 1978, in force 1 July 1978 (hereinafter 'ICJ Rules') ('After hearing the parties, the Court shall give its decision in the form of a judgment, by which it shall either uphold the objection, reject it, or declare that the objection does not possess, in the circumstances of the case, an exclusively preliminary character'); ECHR, art. 29 (allowing, under certain circumstances, separate decisions on admissibility and merits).

11 See ECHR, art. 28(1)(b) (a Committee may declare a case admissible and 'render at the same time a judgment on the merits, if the underlying question in the case, concerning the interpretation or the application of the Convention or the Protocols thereto, is already the subject of well-established case law of the Court').

questions, and the ability of international courts to neatly separate the proceedings dealing with each set of questions. In the *Military and Paramilitary Activities in Nicaragua* case, the International Court of Justice (ICJ) was confronted with a United States objection to its jurisdiction based on a reservation (the 'Vandenberg Amendment'), excluding from the scope of the American optional clause declaration 'disputes arising under a multilateral treaty, unless (1) all parties to the treaty affected by the decision are also parties to the case before the Court, or (2) the United States of America specially agrees to jurisdiction'.[12] Although, the objection was raised by the United States in the jurisdictional phase of the proceedings (preliminary objections), the Court was of a view that given the nature of the reservation, it can only appreciate the need to apply its specific terms when dealing with the merits of the case. This is because identification of the parties affected by the decision, whose participation in the case is required, can only occur after the general contours of the decision and its ensuing effects on the substantive rights and obligations of third parties have been determined (at least in a *prima facie* manner):

> [I]t is only when the general lines of the judgment to be given become clear that the States 'affected' could be identified.[13]

In such circumstances, the Court appears to have had no choice but to rule that the objection to jurisdiction does not have an exclusively preliminary character (pursuant to Rule 79 of the Rules of Court)[14] and to join, in effect, the jurisdictional and substantive stages of the procedure.

At the merits stage of the *Military and Paramilitary Activities in Nicaragua* case, after establishing *prima facie* that the United States had used force against Nicaragua, and after noting that the United States' collective self-defence claim necessarily affected one or more of the neighbouring states on whose behalf self-defence was allegedly exercised, the Court upheld the United States jurisdictional objection. It consequently dismissed those parts of the case based on two

[12] Seventy-ninth US Congress, Acceptance of Compulsory Jurisdiction of International Court of Justice, Senate Res. 196, 2 August 1946.

[13] *Military and Paramilitary Activities in and against Nicaragua* (*Nicaragua* v. *US*), 1984 ICJ 392, 425.

[14] ICJ Rules, Rule 79(7). Rule 79 was amended in 2005, and the relevant sub-section is now Rule 79(9).

relevant multilateral treaties – the United Nations Charter and the Organization of American States Charter.[15] This back-and-forth movement between jurisdictional and substantive issues underscores their intertwined nature in the circumstances of the case.

Another example of jurisdictional and substantive questions intertwined with one another can be found in the ICJ's *Anglo-Iranian Oil* (1952) judgment on preliminary objections, where the Court held, *inter alia*, that a certain concession contract concluded between Iran and a United Kingdom corporation (with the British government's involvement) cannot serve as the basis for the Court's jurisdiction. This is because the United Kingdom was not a formal party to the agreement, and as a result, 'there is no privity of contract between the Government of Iran and the Government of the United Kingdom'.[16] The holding was criticized by Judge Read – one of the dissenting judges – who opined that the United Kingdom's claim that the private concession contract also constituted an implied agreement between the two governments comprised an essential part of its position on the merits of the case. He was therefore of the opinion that the Court should not have dismissed a claim concerning the merits of the case in the jurisdictional phase of the proceedings:

> [T]he Court is not competent, in preliminary proceedings and under the relevant provisions of the Statute and Rules, to decide whether or not an international agreement arose between the two Governments in 1933, one fully operative as creating an obligation in international law. I have reached the conclusion that the competence of the Court, at this stage, is limited to deciding whether the alleged international agreement, assuming that the United Kingdom's contentions as regards its nature and scope are well founded, is a treaty or convention within the meaning of the Declaration.[17]

In other words, Judge Read advocated a procedural rule offering to take at the jurisdictional stage of the proceedings the applicant's

[15] *Military and Paramilitary Activities in and against Nicaragua* (*Nicaragua* v. *US*), 1986 ICJ 3, 37–38. In the end, however, the dismissal of those parts of the claim did not prove to be very significant, since the Court held that parallel norms existed under customary international law, untouched by the multilateral treaties reservation (*Ibid.*, at 97).

[16] *Anglo-Iranian Oil* (*UK* v. *Iran*), 1952 ICJ 93, 112.

[17] *Ibid.*, 1952 ICJ 142, 149 (dissenting opinion of Judge Read).

factual and legal contentions at their highest.[18] Such a position would limit the Court's ability to preliminarily dispose of cases, even if they are based on relatively weak substantive claims, which the Court would most probably find to fall outside its jurisdiction *ratione materiae.*

A variant of the approach proposed by Read was applied by the ICJ in its decision on the second phase of *South West Africa* (1966), where it has held that the conclusion reached in the first phase of the proceedings – that is, that the South West Africa League of Nations Mandate survived the demise of the League – was only provisional in nature:

> [The] 1962 decision on the question of competence was equally given without prejudice to that of the survival of the Mandate, which is a question appertaining to the merits of the case. It was not in issue in 1962, except in the sense that survival had to be assumed for the purpose of determining the purely jurisdictional issue which was all that was then before the Court.[19]

In fact, the ICJ appeared to be of the view that decisions on jurisdiction cannot generate a preclusive effect with relations to questions of merits, regardless of the manner in which the Court in fact treated such issues in the jurisdictional phase of the proceedings:

> [A] decision on a preliminary objection can never be preclusive of a matter appertaining to the merits, whether or not it has in fact been dealt with in connection with the preliminary objection.[20]

From an analytical point of view, there is much to commend about the treatment of questions of merits in connection with objections to jurisdiction, in the manner which has been advocated by Judge Read and endorsed, in effect, by the ICJ in *South West Africa.* Such an approach sharply distinguishes between different stages of proceedings and allows international courts to separate questions relating to their power to adjudicate disputes from questions relating to the outcome of the adjudicative process. It also ensures that questions relating to the merits of the case are fully argued by the parties, and fully considered by the court in the substantive phase of the proceedings.

[18] *Cf. R.* v. *Galbraith* [1981] WLR 1039, 1042 (Crim. App.) (Eng.) ('Where the judge come to the conclusion that the prosecution evidence, taken at its highest, is such that a jury properly directed could not properly convict upon it, it is his duty, upon the submission being made, to stop the case').

[19] *South West Africa* (*Ethiopia* v. *South Africa; Liberia* v. *South Africa),* 1966 ICJ 6, 19.

[20] *Ibid.*, at 37.

Still, following Judge Read's approach to the treatment of substantive issues in preliminary proceedings on jurisdiction may prove to be quite cumbersome from a procedural perspective, as it may require an international court to fully adjudicate the merits of the case, notwithstanding the great likelihood that the claim would fail. Granting judges discretionary powers to consider questions of merits at the jurisdictional phase of the proceedings and to preliminarily dismiss cases on the basis of the clear inability of the applicant party to substantiate a weak factual and legal claim could thus save precious time and resources for the relevant court. Arguably, it could also save time and resources for the disputing parties. It is arguably for these procedural efficiency reasons that some international courts have been explicitly invested with power of discretion in deciding whether or not to preliminarily reject applications that appear weak on their substance.

Human rights bodies' approach to questions of jurisdiction and substance

Indeed, the approach of human rights judicial and quasi-judicial bodies to the separation of questions of jurisdiction from questions relating to the merits of the cases before them has been less clear-cut than that of the ICJ. For example, article 35 of the European Convention authorizes the European Convention on Human Rights (ECtHR) to reject applications which are incompatible with the Convention or manifestly ill-founded. This confers on the Court (and, before 1998, on the Commission) the power to preliminarily dismiss applications which are clearly without merit, either because they claim legal rights which the European Convention does not provide or because they claim violations without offering evidence that could substantiate them.[21] It is interesting to note that Protocol 14 of the Convention granted the ECtHR – probably the most overburdened international court in the world – another legal authority which further erodes the distinction between questions of jurisdiction and the merits. Under article 28(2)(b) of the European Convention, a committee of judges may

[21] ECHR, art. 35 ('the application is incompatible with the provisions of the Convention or the Protocols thereto, manifestly ill-founded, or an abuse of the right of individual application'). The provision was meant to allow the summary dismissal of applications that are 'fantastic' and not 'serious complaints'. Council of Europe – Registry of the European Court of Human Rights, *Preparatory Work on Articles 26–27 of the European Convention on Human Rights*, 23 October 1970, COE Doc. CDH (70) 30, at 10. For similar provisions, see ACHR, art. 47(b)-(c); African Charter on Human and Peoples' Rights, Nairobi, 27 June 1981, in force 21 October 1986, art. 56(2),(4), 21 ILM (1982) 58.

declare an application admissible and render at the same time a judgment on the merits, if the underlying question in the case, concerning the interpretation or the application of the Convention or the Protocols thereto, is already the subject of well-established case-law of the Court.

This implies that 'easy cases' may be summarily disposed of at the jurisdictional stage in a 'simplified and accelerated procedure'.[22]

The United Nations Human Rights Committee, another human rights monitoring body, is also authorized to summarily dismiss communication by alleged victims for their incompatibility with the Covenant.[23] In practice, the Committee has developed a jurisprudence introducing a requirement of factual substantiation of the claims as a condition of admissibility,[24] and the Committee's Rules of Procedure now reflect this standard.[25] Since the Committee tends to join proceedings on admissibility (including the review of possible grounds for lack of jurisdiction and inadmissibility) to proceedings on the merits of communications, it often enjoys rather broad discretion in dismissing a factually weak claim for lack of substantiation or for no proof of a violation. In practical terms, it appears to make little difference which path is used to dismiss the communication. In fact, it is the move away from bifurcated proceedings, containing separate jurisdictional and substantive sets of arguments, which renders the analytical distinction between questions of jurisdiction and merits one of limited practical significance.

Inability to invoke substantive rights

Instances of *prima facie* incompatibility with the governing legal text or lack of factual substantiation represent one set of situations in which international courts may sometimes invoke questions of merits

[22] Council of Europe, *Explanatory Report to Protocol No. 14 to the European Convention for the Protection of Human Rights and Fundamental Freedoms, amending the Control System of the Convention*, 12 May 2009, ETS 194, at para 69.

[23] Optional Protocol to the ICCPR, art. 3.

[24] See HRC, *D.B.* v. *Canada*, Communication No. 15/1977, para. 20, U.N. Doc. CCPR/C/OP/1 (1984); Tom Zwart, *The Admissibility of Human Rights Petitions: The Case Law of the European Commission of Human Rights and the Human Rights Committee* (Dordrecht: Martinus Nijhoff Publishers, 1994), pp. 144–146. The Committee typically reads the requirement of sufficient substantiation into the term 'claim' in art. 2 of the Optional Protocol.

[25] Human Rights Committee, Rule of Procedure (as amended on 11 January 2012), Rule 96(b),UN Doc. CCPR/C.3/Rev.10 (2012).

in the jurisdictional phase of the proceedings. Another potential set of situations, which also demonstrate the interconnectedness of certain questions of jurisdiction and merits, involves the jurisdictional implications of a definitive finding by an international court that the rights, which the applicant party claims to have been violated, were not protected by the governing instrument or did not give the applicant a right of action against the respondent party.

Analytically, it is possible to draw a distinction between *prima facie* findings on substantive questions of fact and law and eventual findings thereon, as the ICJ has done in the second phase of *South West Africa*:

> [A] distinction has to be made between, on the one hand, the right to activate a court and the right of the court to examine the merits of the claim, – and, on the other, the plaintiff party's legal right in respect of the subject-matter of that which it claims, which would have to be established to the satisfaction of the Court.[26]

Indeed, in the first phase of the proceedings, the Court found strong support in the history, context and purpose and subsequent practice involving the Mandate for South West Africa for the right of League of Nations member states to bring legal action to enforce the Mandate, which survived the demise of the League.[27] Nevertheless, in the second phase of the proceedings the Court emphasized the non-preclusive attributes of the decision on jurisdiction: its provisional nature and its inability to prejudge the merits of the case.[28] This subtle distinction between findings reached for the purpose of establishing the applicants' legal interest in bringing the claim and their legal interest in prevailing therein, appears to correspond to the distinction between *prima facie* and eventual findings on the merits.

[26] *South West Africa* (*Ethiopia* v. *South Africa*), 1966 ICJ 6, at 39.

[27] *South West Africa* (*Ethiopia* v. *South Africa*), 1962 ICJ 319, at 335–342 (Preliminary Objections).

[28] *South West Africa* (*Ethiopia* v. *South Africa*), 1966 ICJ 6, at 37 ('It may occur that a judgment on a preliminary objection touches on a point of merits, but this it can do only in a provisional way, to the extent necessary for deciding the question raised by the preliminary objection. Any finding on the point of merits therefore, ranks simply as part of the motivation of the decision on the preliminary objection, and not as the object of that decision. It cannot rank as a final decision on the point of merits involved'); *Ibid.*, at 38 ('decisions of an interlocutory character cannot pre-judge questions of merits').

Not all international courts maintain a sharp distinction between the right to activate the court – based on a *prima facie* legal claim – and the eventual disposition of the merits of the legal claim. For instance, the ECtHR has sometimes chosen to present its conclusion that an applicant party is unable to invoke a substantive right against the respondent party as one of jurisdiction, rather than as a conclusion pertaining to the merits of the case. This is notwithstanding the fact that such conclusions were often reached after an elaborate analysis of the governing legal instruments, which invited comprehensive argumentation on the substantive factual and legal issues raised in the case.

For example, the ECtHR held in its 2001 *Bankovic* decision that an application brought by relatives of aerial bombing victims against a number of NATO member states, alleging their responsibility for the attack on a television station in Belgrade on 23 April 1999, is inadmissible under article 35(3)-(4) of the European Convention because of the lack of a jurisdictional link between the victims and the respondent states.[29] In the same vein, the Court held in its 2007 *Behrami* decision that an application brought by relatives of victims of explosive remnants of war and individuals detained without trial against states contributing forces to the international presence in Kosovo is 'incompatible *ratione personae* with the provisions of the Convention', since it was the United Nations and not the individual member states who bore responsibility for the harms suffered by the applicants and their relatives.[30]

In both cases, the decision rendered by the Court did not really revolve around questions of jurisdiction – that is, whether the Court was authorized to adjudicate the application, but rather around questions relating to the merits of the case – that is, whether the respondent states had, in the circumstances of the cases, assumed legal obligations under the Convention towards the applicants.[31]

[29] *Bankovic* v. *Belgium*, App. No. 52207/99, ECtHR decision of 12 December 2001, para 85.

[30] *Behrami* v. *France*, App. No. 71412/01, ECtHR decision of 2 May 2007, para 152.

[31] *Bankovic*, note 29, at para 82 ('The Court is not therefore persuaded that there was any jurisdictional link between the persons who were victims of the act complained of and the respondent States. Accordingly, it is not satisfied that the applicants and their deceased relatives were capable of coming within the jurisdiction of the respondent States on account of the extra-territorial act in question'); *Behrami*, note 30, at para 144 ('It is therefore the case that the impugned action and inaction are, in principle, attributable to the UN. It is, moreover, clear that the UN has a legal personality separate from that of its

Significantly, both decisions were reached after the relevant issues had been fully argued before the Court, and after it undertook an extensive investigation of the legal obligations introduced by the European Convention of Human Rights (ECHR) and applied them to the facts of the case. Such a process of investigation of facts and law constitutes the essence of legal adjudication, and to treat it as a pure matter of jurisdiction might have implied that the Court conducted a substantive adjudicative exercise without first establishing its authority to do so.

Indeed, the questions of fact and law adjudicated in *Bankovic* and *Behrami* are more closely analogous to the question of the existence of a legal right to rely on the substantive obligations of the Mandate definitively determined by the ICJ in the second phase of the *South West Africa* case than to the procedural question of legal standing to bring a claim to the Court addressed in the first phase of the proceedings. Note that the ICJ dismissed the case in the *South West Africa* case (second phase) after finding that the applicant parties failed to establish a substantive aspect of the case having a preliminary character – a failure that rendered it redundant to discuss other substantive aspects of the case. The dismissal of a case on the basis of a substantive question of a preliminary character has been described by Judge Fitzmaurice in his separate opinion in the *Northern Cameroons* case as analytically different from dismissal because of a lack of jurisdiction nor because of a lack of judicial propriety.[32] In the same vein, it may be claimed that the decisions of the ECtHR in *Bankovic* and *Behrami* should not be viewed as truly preliminary, notwithstanding their framing as admissibility proceedings (revolving around the compatibility of the application with the ECHR). Moreover, they should not be regarded as involving a question of jurisdiction just because of the allusion by the Court to the term jurisdiction in order to describe the substantive scope of application of the ECHR.

With regard to the preliminary nature of the proceedings, I have already noted that the ECtHR is authorized under the ECHR to reject applications preliminarily if they are 'incompatible with

member states [*The Reparations case*, ICJ Reports 1949] and that that organisation is not a Contracting Party to the Convention').

32 *Northern Cameroons* (*Cameroon* v. *UK*), 1963 ICJ 15, 103 (separate opinion of Judge Fitzmaurice). For a discussion, see Brian Flemming, 'Note: Case Concerning the Northern Cameroons (Cameroon v. United Kingdom), Preliminary Objections' (1964) 2 Canadian YB Int'l Law 215, 229–230.

the provisions of the Convention' or 'manifestly ill-founded'.[33] Furthermore, the Convention authorizes the Court to address admissibility questions 'at any stage of the proceedings'.[34] Thus, it appears that there is nothing in the Convention to bar the Court from treating substantive questions of merits having a preliminary character, such as the scope of application of the ECHR or the division of responsibilities in peacekeeping operations between the United Nations and the participating member states (which is analogous to the question of substantive legal relations raised in *South West Africa*), as part of the Court's treatment of questions of admissibility. Once the Court has reached the conclusion that the application is devoid of legal merit or lacks factual substantiation, it may bring the proceedings to an end, by declaring them inadmissible. While from an analytical point of view, the Court has extended in the two decisions the concept of inadmissibility so as to encompass situations where the applicants have failed to definitively establish a key element of their claim on the merits (i.e. going beyond *prima facie* legal incompatibility or lack of factual substantiation), in practical terms, the distinction between failure to establish substantive aspects in a *prima facie* and definitive manner appears to play a modest role only in the jurisdictional configuration of the ECtHR.

With regard to the use of the term 'jurisdiction' in both ECtHR decisions,[35] it should be noted that the term has been employed in a context altogether different than the one used in this book. It does not connote the power of the Court to adjudicate, but rather the degree of authority and control exercised by states over individuals who claim to be victims of human rights violations. Admittedly, the two meanings of jurisdiction may be connected at times – an act or omission falling outside the jurisdiction of a state, may, like in cases involving lack of jurisdiction for the court in question, result in the dismissal of a claim against that state. Still, questions of 'state

[33] ECHR, art. 35(3)(a). [34] ECHR, art. 35(4).

[35] *Bankovic*, note 29, at para. 54 ('It considers that the essential question to be examined therefore is whether the applicants and their deceased relatives were, as a result of that extra-territorial act, capable of falling within the jurisdiction of the respondent States'); *Behrami*, note 30, at para 71 ('The Court therefore considers that the question raised by the present cases is, less whether the respondent States exercised extra-territorial jurisdiction in Kosovo but far more centrally, whether this Court is competent to examine under the Convention those States' contribution to the civil and security presences which did exercise the relevant control of Kosovo').

jurisdiction' are simply one set of elements potentially comprising the merits of the claim (like attribution, deviation from binding legal standards, etc.), and have nothing uniquely 'jurisdictional' about them as far as the power of courts to adjudicate are concerned.

In summary, one may note that the broad powers entertained by the ECtHR to declare applications inadmissible and to control the order of the proceedings[36] afford it with considerable discretion as to how to treat questions of a substantive nature, having a preliminary character. Arguably, considerations of judicial economy may have led the Court in both the *Bankovic* and *Behrami* to deal with the scope of obligations introduced by the Convention as part of the initial stage of the proceedings, dealing with the admissibility of the application.[37] To the extent that the procedural rights of the parties have not been adversely affected by the examination of substantive questions at the admissibility phase, there seem to be few principled grounds for objecting to this practice.

It is somewhat more difficult, however, to justify from a procedural point of view the ICJ's holding in the provisional measures phase of *Use of Force (NATO)* that the Court did not have *prima facie* jurisdiction, because it did not gain the impression that the attacks described by Yugoslavia were intended to destroy a group as required by the Genocide Convention.[38] There is little doubt in my eyes that the genocide part of Yugoslavia's claim was ill-founded (perhaps even amounting to an *abus de droit*)[39] and that an international court authorized to preliminarily reject frivolous claims should have done so. However, the ICJ does not have under its Statute an explicit power

[36] See also European Court of Human Rights, Rules of Court, Rule 54A, 1 July 2014 (power to join proceedings on admissibility with proceedings on the merits).

[37] *Cf. Northern Cameroons* (*Cameroon* v. *UK*), 1963 ICJ 15, at 105 (separate opinion of Judge Fitzmaurice) ('There would clearly be an element of absurdity in the Court going through all the motions of establishing its jurisdiction, if it considered it must then in any event decline to examine the claim on this ground, however competent it might be to do so').

[38] *Legality of Use of Force* (*Yugoslavia* v. *Belgium*), 1999 ICJ 124, 138 (provisional measures) ('Whereas the Court is therefore not in a position to find, at this stage of the proceedings, that the acts imputed by Yugoslavia to the Respondent are capable of coming within the provisions of the Genocide Convention; and whereas Article IX of the Convention, invoked by Yugoslavia, cannot accordingly constitute a basis on which the jurisdiction of the Court could prima facie be founded in this case').

[39] See e.g. Bin Cheng, *General Principles of Law as Applied by International Courts and Tribunals* (Cambridge: Cambridge University Press, 1953), pp. 121–122.

to summarily dismiss claims due to their frivolousness. Furthermore, unlike some domestic courts, the ICJ is not authorized to deny the grant of provisional measures based on the low likelihood of the applicant prevailing on the merits.[40] Instead, it can only consider whether *prima facie* jurisdiction exists.[41]

Hence, it is questionable whether it was proper for the ICJ to express a view on the merits of the *Use of Force (NATO)* case – that is, alluding to the *prima facie* lack of intent to destroy a group on the part of NATO member states – in the context of an examination of whether it has *prima facie* jurisdiction over the claim for the purposes of considering whether to issue provisional measures.[42] Ultimately, I believe that the Court was right in rejecting the request for provisional measures, but not because of lack of *prima facie* jurisdiction, but rather as part of its inherent power to reject abusive motions.[43] Interestingly enough, the 2004 judgment on preliminary objections dismissed Yugoslavia's claims on grounds

[40] *Cf. Doran* v. *Salem Inn, Inc.*, 422 U.S. 922 (1975) ('The traditional standard for granting a preliminary injunction requires the plaintiff to show that in the absence of its issuance he will suffer irreparable injury and also that he is likely to prevail on the merits').

[41] The power of the ICJ to deny provisional measures in cases of *prima facie* lack of jurisdiction has been affirmed in numerous judgments. See e.g. *Anglo-Iranian Oil Co. (UK* v. *Iran)*, 1951 ICJ 89, 93 (provisional measures) ('it cannot be accepted a priori that a claim based on such a complaint falls completely outside the scope of international jurisdiction'); *Diplomatic and Consular Staff in Tehran (US* v. *Iran)*, 1979 ICJ 6, 13 (provisional measures) ('Whereas on the request for provisional measures in the present case the Court ought to indicate such measures only if the provisions invoked by the Applicant appear, prima facie, to afford a basis on which the jurisdiction of the Court might be founded'). See generally Shabtai Rosenne, *Provisional Measures in International Law: The International Court of Justice and the International Tribunal for the Law of the Sea* (Oxford: Oxford University, 2005).

[42] See *Legality of Use of Force*, 1999 ICJ at 241 (dissenting opinion of *ad hoc* judge Kreca) ('Of the utmost importance is the fact that, in the incidental proceedings, the Court cannot and should not concern itself with the definitive qualification of the intent to impose upon the group conditions in which the survival of the group is threatened. Having in mind the purpose of provisional measures, it can be said that at this stage of the proceedings it is sufficient to establish that, in the conditions of intensive bombing, there is an objective risk of bring about conditions in which the survival of the group is threatened').

[43] For a discussion, see Chester Brown, *A Common Law of International Adjudication* (New York: Oxford University Press, 2007), p. 124 *et seq.*; Karin Oellers-Frahm, 'Expanding the Competence to Issue Provisional Measures – Strengthening the International Judicial Function' (2011) 12 GERMAN L.J. 1279, 1281.

unrelated to the applicability of the Genocide Convention or to any of the other grounds discussed in the 1999 decision.[44]

Difficulty in classifying claims as procedural or substantive in nature

Another category of interactions between jurisdictional provisions and substantive law involves cases in which there is lack of clarity as to whether a specific legal requirement, upon which the success of the claim rests, is jurisdictional or substantive in nature. Such a question arises most frequently in diplomatic protection cases, where exhaustion of local remedies has sometimes been regarded by international courts as a jurisdictional precondition attaching to a specific category of cases brought by states on behalf of their nationals or by the directly concerned individual, and sometimes described as a substantive element in the claim, in whose absence no violation of international law has occurred.[45]

For instance, an ICSID arbitral tribunal held in *Loewe* v. *United States* that

> [t]he local remedies rule which requires a party complaining of a breach of international law by a State to exhaust the local remedies in that State before the party can raise the complaint at the level of international law is procedural in character.[46]

At the same time, the tribunal took the view that lack of exhaustion may sometimes constitute a defence against certain substantive claims (such as denial of justice) in the sense that no violation of an international law obligation has occurred without exhaustion.[47] In

[44] *Legality of Use of Force*, 2004 ICJ 279, 327–328.

[45] See e.g. James E S Fawcett, 'The Exhaustion of Local Remedies: Substance or Procedure?' (1954) 31 Brit. Y.B. Int'l L. 452, 452–458; Silvia S'Ascoli and Kathrin Maria Scherr, 'The Rule of Prior Exhaustion of Local Remedies in the International Law Doctrine and its Application in the Specific Context of Human Rights Protection', EUI Working Papers, Law 2007/2, at 2–5.

[46] *The Loewen Group, Inc.* v. *USA*, Case No. ARB(AF)/98/3, Award of 26 June 2003, para. 149.

[47] *Ibid.*, at para 154 ('No instance has been drawn to our attention in which an international tribunal has held a State responsible for a breach of international law constituted by a lower court decision when there was available an effective and adequate appeal within the State's legal system').

ELSI, the ICJ adopted a middle ground position suggesting that exhaustion is not a question of jurisdiction, but rather of admissibility, and it should therefore be decided at the beginning of the merits stage.[48] This can be understood either as a general statement in favour of the possibility of treating some questions of admissibility at the merits stage of the proceedings, while retaining the distinction between the exhaustion rule and the merits of the case,[49] or as an expression of support for treating the exhaustion rule as a question of substance, that is, a substantive question of an preliminary character.

The differences in classification of an objection in the nature of lack of exhaustion of local remedies may affect not only the procedural stage of litigation in which the questions should be discussed but also the allocation of burdens of proof among the litigating parties (e.g. the requirement for the applicant to negate a substantive defence and for the respondent to establish a procedural objection).[50] Furthermore, the willingness of an international court to attribute to the respondent state an implicit intent to waive the requirement of exhaustion, or to apply a rule of estoppel to bar it from invoking it, may be affected by its classification as procedural or substantive. For instance, the decision of the ECtHR in *Aksoy* v. *Turkey* to regard an interview with a prosecutor in which signs of physical torture were visible as a form of exhaustion may reflect a flexible approach towards the exhaustion rule which treats lack of exhaustion as a curable flaw of a procedural

48 *Elettronica Sicula S.p.A. (ELSI)* (*USA* v. *Italy*), 1989 ICJ 15, 42:

> While the jurisdiction of the Chamber is not in doubt, an objection to the admissibility of the present case was entered by Italy in its Counter Memorial, on the ground of an alleged failure of the two United States corporations, Raytheon and Machlett, on whose behalf the United States claim is brought, to exhaust the local remedies available to them in Italy. This objection, which the Parties agreed should be heard and determined in the framework of the merits, must, therefore, be considered at the outset.

49 International Law Commission, Draft Articles on State Responsibility for Internationally Wrongful Acts with Commentaries (2001) 121 (commentary to art. 44: 'The Chamber thus treated the exhaustion of local remedies as being distinct, in principle, from "the merits of the case"').

50 Sean D Murphy, 'The ELSI Case: An Investment Dispute at the International Court of Justice' (1991) 16 Yale J. Int'l L. 391, 413 at n 97; Thomas Haesler, *The Exhaustion of Local Remedies in the Case Law of International Courts and Tribunals* (Leiden: A. W. Sijthoff, 1968), pp. 57–59.

nature.[51] In the same vein, one may regard the recent decision of the Human Rights Committee in *Husseini* v. *Denmark* to attribute to the respondent state an intent to waive the duty to exhaust local remedies when lack of exhaustion has been argued only implicitly and not explicitly, as applying a procedural burden of proof on the respondent state to show that its jurisdictional objection has been clearly made.[52]

Still, the two investment disputes mentioned earlier – *Loewen* and *ELSI* – represent a more stringent approach to the exhaustion rule, perhaps suggesting that it ought to be regarded as substantive in nature. In *Loewen*, the tribunal has held that failure of the investor to explain his reasons for not exhausting a specific remedy prevents it from finding a substantive violation of international law,[53] and in *ELSI* the Court took the view that the exhaustion rule cannot be implicitly waived.[54]

I should note that, according to the approach I present in this book, the exhaustion rule is to be regarded, depending on the overarching legal context, either as a jurisdictional condition or as a substantive law requirement – for example, an element in a denial of justice claim. This means that under no circumstances do international courts enjoy discretion to dispense with the rule altogether, since it is either a prerequisite for the exercise of judicial power or for establishing a substantive violation. Still, what constitutes an effective remedy for the purpose of applying the exhaustion rule will inevitably be subject to some interpretative discretion and certain discretion in the evaluation of the available local remedies. Moreover, in a consent-based system,

[51] *Aksoy* v. *Turkey*, App. No, 21987/93, 1996-IV EHRR (No. 26), para 53 ('[the exhaustion rule] must be applied with some degree of flexibility and without excessive formalism').

[52] HRC, *Husseini* v. *Denmark*, Communication No. 2243/2013, para 8.3, U.N. Doc. CCPR/C/112/D/2243/2013 (2014). For criticism, see *Ibid.*, Joint opinion of Committee members Shany and Seetulsingh (dissenting).

[53] *Loewen*, note 46, at paras 215–217:

> Loewen failed to present evidence disclosing its reasons for entering into the settlement agreement in preference to pursuing other options, in particular the Supreme Court option which it had under active consideration and preparation until the settlement agreement was reached. It is a matter on which the onus of proof rested with Loewen . . . Accordingly, our conclusion is that Loewen failed to pursue its domestic remedies, notably the Supreme Court option and that, in consequence, Loewen has not shown a violation of customary international law and a violation of NAFTA for which Respondent is responsible.

[54] *Elettronica Sicula S.p.A. (ELSI)* (*USA* v. *Italy*), 1989 ICJ 15, 42.

respondent states may waive – explicitly or implicitly – jurisdictional conditions that restrict the scope of their consent to jurisdiction, and are limited in the invocation of their procedural and substantive rights by general principles of law, including the principle of estoppel.[55] Thus, a decision by the respondent party to waive the need for exhaustion of local remedies should be respected by the international court before which the relevant case is adjudicated.

[55] Cheng, note 39, at pp. 143–144.

8

International court decisions on jurisdiction as a form of category-based case selection

The duty to exercise jurisdiction

A key aspect of the law governing the jurisdiction of international courts is the duty to exercise it, which is implicitly, and at times explicitly, specified in the instrument granting them legal authority to adjudicate.[1] International courts serve in this respect as agents (or trustees) on behalf of their two sets of principals – the mandate providers and the parties to the dispute – who expect them to adjudicate cases properly referred to them. Such expectations are reflective of a legal regime in which disputing parties have, following the fulfilment of certain prerequisites, a right to adjudicate; and discretionary denial of jurisdiction by an international court may render illusory this parties' right. Thus, unless international courts can identify a valid reason not to exercise their jurisdiction, they must exercise it,[2]

1 See e.g. ICJ Statute, art. 36(1) ('The jurisdiction of the Court comprises all cases which the parties refer to it'), art. 38(1) ('The Court, whose function is to decide in accordance with international law such disputes as are submitted to it, *shall* apply . . .'). *Cf. ibid.*, art. 65(1) ('The Court *may* give an advisory opinion on any legal question at the request of whatever body may be authorised by or in accordance with the Charter of the United Nations to make such a request') (emphasis added). See also DSU, art. 7 (enumerating terms of reference of Dispute Settlement Body panels); the ICSID Convention, art. 42(1) ('The Tribunal *shall* decide a dispute in accordance with such rules of law as may be agreed by the parties') (emphasis added); TFEU, art. 263 ('The Court of Justice of the European Union *shall* review the legality of legislative acts, of acts of the Council, of the Commission and of the European Central Bank') (emphasis added).

2 *Continental Shelf (Libya/Malta)*, 1985 ICJ 13, 23 ('The Court must not exceed the jurisdiction conferred upon it by the Parties, but it must also exercise that jurisdiction to its full extent').

regardless of any implications this may have on the court's workload, its political standing in the world, or internal divisions among the judges.

The proposition that international courts must, as a rule, exercise the jurisdiction conferred upon them enjoys support in the case law of international courts. For example, an International Centre for the Settlement of Investment Disputes (ICSID) *ad hoc* committee held in *Vivendi* v. *Argentina* that:

> It is settled, and neither party disputes, that an ICSID tribunal commits an excess of powers not only if it exercises a jurisdiction which it does not have under the relevant agreement or treaty and the ICSID Convention, read together, but also if it fails to exercise a jurisdiction which it possesses under those instruments.[3]

In the same vein, the World Trade Organization (WTO) Appellate Body (AB) has emphasized that the Dispute Settlement Body adjudicators have no discretion on whether or not to hear a case validly referred to them just because another, more appropriate, adjudication forum exists:

> The fact that a Member may initiate a WTO dispute whenever it considers that 'any benefits accruing to [that Member] are being impaired by measures taken by another Member' implies that that Member is *entitled* to a ruling by a WTO panel. A decision by a panel to decline to exercise validly established jurisdiction would seem to 'diminish' the right of a complaining Member to 'seek the redress of a violation of obligations' within the meaning of Article 23 of the DSU, and to bring a dispute pursuant to Article 3.3 of the DSU. This would not be consistent with a panel's obligations under Articles 3.2 and 19.2 of the DSU. We see no reason, therefore, to disagree with the Panel's statement that a WTO panel 'would seem ... not to be in a position to choose freely whether or not to exercise its jurisdiction'.[4]

It may be noted that the International Court of Justice (ICJ) has emphasized in a number of advisory opinions that its advisory competence is discretionary in nature and that it may decline jurisdiction for compelling reasons of impropriety.[5] Arguably, the reference to

[3] *Compañía de Aguas del Aconquija S.A. and Vivendi Universal* v. *Argentina*, Case No. ARB/97/3, Decision on Annulment of 3 June 2002 (ICSID *ad hoc* Committee), at para 86.

[4] *Mexico – Tax Measures on Soft Drinks and Other Beverages*, Report of the AB of 6 March 2006, WTO Doc. WT/DS308/AB/R, at paras 52–53.

[5] See e.g. *Interpretation of Peace Treaty with Bulgaria, Hungary and Romania*, 1950 ICJ 65, 72 (first phase) ('Article 65 of the Statute is permissive. It gives the Court the

the Court's power to decline to exercise its advisory power underscores its obligation to exercise its adjudicative power in contentious cases.

The significance of case selection

The non-discretionary nature of the duty of international courts to exercise jurisdiction over cases validly referred to adjudication appears to deprive them of the power to engage in case selection. Yet without case selection, the task of international courts might become much more difficult. This is because through control of their dockets international courts can prioritize important cases with significant implications for attainment of the court's goals, and avoid dealing with cases which the court is ill-equipped to adjudicate or which could result in harmful consequences for itself or the legal regime it serves.[6]

In practice, the process of establishing the jurisdiction of international courts over disputes referred to them inevitably contains strong discretionary features. Through the discretion they exercise at a number of critical legal junctures that present themselves in the adjudicative procedure, international courts are able to exercise some degree of case selection, which tends to be category-based and not case-specific, however.

First, I have already discussed earlier the ability of some international courts to determine the sequencing of certain aspects of the case and to deal preliminarily with questions relating to the merits

power to examine whether the circumstances of the case are of such a character as should lead it to decline to answer the Request'); *Legality of the Threat or Use of Nuclear Weapons*, 1996 ICJ 226, 234–235 ('Article 65, paragraph 1, of the Statute provides: 'The Court *may* give an advisory opinion ...' [emphasis added]. This is more than an enabling provision. As the Court has repeatedly emphasised, the Statute leaves a discretion as to whether or not it will give an advisory opinion that has been requested of it, once it has established its competence to do so'). The obligation to exercise jurisdiction has been explicitly recognized by the PCIJ in the *Serbian Loans* case. *The Payment of Various Serbian Loans Issued in France* (*France* v. *Kingdom of the Serbs, Croats and Slovenes*), 1929 PCIJ (ser. A) No. 20/21, at 19 ('When the two States have agreed to have recourse to the Court, the latter's *duty to exercise its jurisdiction* cannot be affected, in the absence of a clause in the Statute on the subject, by the circumstance that the dispute relates to a question of municipal law rather than to a pure matter of fact') (emphasis added).

[6] *Cf.* Doris M Provine, *Case Selection in the US Supreme Court* (Chicago, IL: The University of Chicago Press, 1980), pp. 1–2.

that have a preliminary character. Such discretionary sequencing allows international courts to expand the grounds for summarily dismissing cases without engaging in full treatment of the parties' arguments and to de-prioritize meritless cases.

Secondly, Part III of this book explores grounds of inadmissibility, which allow some international courts to apply their discretion and dismiss cases validly referred to them based on considerations of justice, propriety and judicial economy. International courts whose constitutive instruments contain admissibility provisions are thus constitutionally empowered to engage in discretionary case selection.

Still, the most important occasion for the exercise of judicial discretion in connection with case selection, applied by all international courts, involves the interpretation of the jurisdictional provisions governing their operation.[7] While international courts may not – outside the context of certain rules on admissibility – decline to exercise jurisdiction validly bestowed upon them by citing policy considerations relating to their effectiveness or legitimacy, they may rely on such policy considerations to decide whether they have jurisdiction to begin with. The determination of the court's scope of jurisdiction pursuant to the exercise of interpretive discretion results, in effect, in the retention of certain categories in cases and in the exclusion of other categories – that is, case selection on a category basis.

The list of decisions on jurisdiction, which illustrate the role played by policy considerations in determining the scope of authority of international courts, is too long to be covered exhaustively here. In many, and probably most, of these cases, the policy considerations leading to the jurisdictional decision were not explicitly discussed in the relevant court decision. On some occasions, however – including several ICJ cases – the relevant policy considerations were discussed in relatively explicit terms.

Hence, for example, in its judgment on *Application of the Convention on the Elimination of Racial Discrimination (CERD)* the ICJ held that the term 'dispute . . . which is not settled' – a foundational jurisdictional condition found in article 22 of CERD – implies that the parties are under a duty to exhaust alternative methods of dispute resolution.[8]

[7] Aharon Barak, *Purposive Interpretation in Law* (Princeton, NJ: Princeton University Press, 2005), p. 207.

[8] *Application of the International Convention on the Elimination of All Forms of Racial Discrimination* (*Georgia* v. *Russian Federation*), 2011 ICJ 70, 128.

In support of this outcome, the Court cited, *inter alia*, the following policy arguments:

Such resort fulfils three distinct functions. In the first place, it gives notice to the respondent State that a dispute exists and delimits the scope of the dispute and its subject-matter. The Permanent Court of International Justice was aware of this when it stated in the *Mavrommatis* case that 'before a dispute can be made the subject of an action in law, its subject-matter should have been clearly defined by means of diplomatic negotiations' [cite omitted]. In the second place, it encourages the Parties to attempt to settle their dispute by mutual agreement, thus avoiding recourse to binding third-party adjudication. In the third place, prior resort to negotiations or other methods of peaceful dispute settlement performs an important function in indicating the limit of consent given by States.[9]

Put differently, the interpretation of article 22 embraced by the Court is supported by considerations of judicial economy (the need to delimit the factual and legal questions at dispute before adjudication commences), promoting, more generally, efficiency in the management of international disputes (encouraging non-judicial methods of peaceful dispute settlement as a preferred alternative to adjudication) and judicial legitimacy (ensuring consent to all aspects of the case referred to the Court). Such considerations would underlay, by necessary implications, the application of article 22 to future cases as well, containing similar features (and, arguably, the application of analogous compromissory clauses found in other human rights treaties, as well).[10]

Another example of the role of policy consideration in the interpretation of specific jurisdictional provisions, amounting in effect to category-based case selection, may be found in the ICJ's *Fisheries Jurisdiction* judgment. In that case, the Court considered the role that consent plays in the work of the ICJ, and opted for a canon of

[9] *Ibid.*, at 124–125.

[10] See e.g. Convention against Torture and Other Cruel, Inhuman or Degrading Treatment or Punishment, 10 December 1984, in force 26 June 1987, art. 30, 1465 U.N.T.S. 85; International Convention for the Protection of All Persons from Enforced Disappearance, 20 December 2006, in force 23 December 2010, art. 42, U.N. Doc. A/RES/61/177 (2006). Both treaty provisions use, however, a formulation referring unresolved disputes to arbitration: 'Any dispute between two or more States Parties concerning the interpretation or application of this Convention which cannot be settled through negotiation or by the procedures expressly provided for in this Convention shall, at the request of one of them, be submitted to arbitration.'

interpretation that emphasizes the actual intent of parties that have submitted jurisdictional reservations (subjective consent) over a more objective reading of such instruments, relying when needed also on the relevant *travaux préparatoires*:

> The Court will thus interpret the relevant words of a declaration including a reservation contained therein in a natural and reasonable way, having due regard to the intention of the State concerned at the time when it accepted the compulsory jurisdiction of the Court. The intention of a reserving State may be deduced not only from the text of the relevant clause, but also from the context in which the clause is to be read, and an examination of evidence regarding the circumstances of its preparation and the purposes intended to be served.[11]

It may be speculated that the Court was interested not only in ensuring genuine consent of all parties to its exercise of jurisdiction – a policy consideration related to the need to preserve its source legitimacy (i.e. as an adjudicative institution exercising legal powers actually delegated to it). In all probability, the Court was also weighing strategic considerations of long-term effectiveness: By refusing to construe reservations in a way which deviates from the subjective intent of the reserving party, the ICJ protected its institutional interest in encouraging the submission of declarations of acceptance of its jurisdiction. Had reservations to declarations of acceptance been narrowly construed by the Court – as advocated by the Spain (the applicant state) – respondent states might have decided to withdraw existing declarations, or to refrain from submitting them to begin with. Such an outcome might have led over time to a decrease in the number of cases submitted to the Court.[12]

Still, in some cases, policy considerations other than the need to respect the principle of consent to adjudication appear to have caused the ICJ to assume jurisdiction despite the existence of certain procedural flaws in the process of authorization. For example, in *Military and Paramilitary Activities in Nicaragua*, the Court was willing to downplay the significance of irregularities in the process by which Nicaragua accepted the Court's compulsory jurisdiction under the optional clause (i.e. its failure to send an instrument of ratification), *inter alia* because of considerations of fairness: It was of the view that it

[11] *Fisheries Jurisdiction* (*Spain* v. *Canada*), 1998 ICJ 432, 454.

[12] Interestingly enough, the Court downplayed the significance of considerations of effectiveness, when these conflict with the principle of consent. *Ibid.*, at 455.

would be unfair to prevent Nicaragua from relying on the Court's own publications which listed it as an optional clause state:

> [I]f the Court were to object that Nicaragua ought to have made a declaration under Article 36, paragraph 2, it would be penalizing Nicaragua for having attached undue weight to the information given on that point by the Court and the Secretary-General of the United Nations and, in sum, having (on account of the authority of their sponsors) regarded them as more reliable than they really were.[13]

In other words, the Court seemed to imply that considerations of fairness (good faith reliance on the information published by the Court) may affect the determination of its specific jurisdictional powers, and could justify, in the circumstances of the case, prioritization of substance (intent to accept jurisdiction) over form (submission of a valid declaration of acceptance).

In the same vein, the Court held in *Application of the Genocide Convention (Croatia* v. *Serbia)* that even lack of foundational jurisdiction at the moment of seisin (in the relevant circumstances – the non-membership of Serbia of the ICJ Statute when proceedings were initiated in 1999) may be cured were the applicant able to bring at the time in which jurisdiction was considered a fresh set of proceedings. According to the Court, 'it is not in the interests of the sound administration of justice to compel the applicant to begin the proceedings anew'.[14]

Thus, considerations of judicial economy and 'sound administration of justice' have in this case mitigated in favour of procedural flexibility in applying a jurisdictional provision, allowing the fulfilment of the conditions it introduces at a later-in-time point than the date of initiation of proceedings. This has been presented by the Court – pursuant to the Permanent Court of International Justice's (PCIJ) *Mavrommatis* holding – as a manifestation of the principle that the ICJ is 'not bound to attach to matters of form the same degree of importance which they might possess in municipal law'.[15]

[13] *Military and Paramilitary Activities in and against Nicaragua* (*Nicaragua* v. *US*), 1984 ICJ 392, 412.

[14] *Application of the Convention on the Prevention and Punishment of the Crime of Genocide* (*Croatia* v. *Serbia*), 2008 ICJ 412, 441.

[15] *Ibid.*, at 439. See also *Mavrommatis Palestine Concessions* (*Greece* v. *GB*), 1924 PCIJ (Ser. A) No. 2, at 34 (Objections to Jurisdiction).

Still, in both cases in which the Court has been willing to allow for flexibility in the application of jurisdictional clauses – flexibility in identifying consent to jurisdiction in *Military and Paramilitary Activities in Nicaragua*, and flexibility in determining the decisive moment for verifying the fulfilment of jurisdictional conditions in *Application of the Genocide Convention (Croatia* v. *Serbia)* – it may be speculated that other policy concerns also affected these decisions. For example, in both cases, it may have been the desire of the Court to exercise jurisdiction over 'high politics' disputes,[16] underscoring thereby its relevance in use of force cases and its potential contribution to the maintenance of international peace and security.[17] Such a hypothesis is consistent with other manifestations of what can be regarded as increased assertiveness by the ICJ in cases relating to the maintenance of international peace and security. For instance, the Court retained jurisdiction in the 2007 *Application of the Genocide Convention (Bosnia* v. *Serbia)* case notwithstanding a serious challenge to its foundational jurisdiction;[18] and in the 2003 *Oil Platforms* case it applied the principles of *jus ad bellum* in circumstances where such an application was immaterial to the disposition of the case (thus constituting, in effect, *obiter dicta*).[19] Furthermore,

16 On the distinction between 'high politics' and 'low politics', see e.g. Robert S Jordan, *International Organizations: A Comparative Approach to the Management of Conflict* (Westport, CT: Greenwood Publishing Group, 2001), p. 23; Brigid Starkey *et al.*, *International Negotiation in a Complex World*, 3rd edn. (Lanham, MD: Rowman & Littlefield Publishers, 2010), pp. 89–91.

17 See in another context, *Diplomatic and Consular Staff in Tehran* (*US* v. *Iran*), 1980 ICJ 3, 22 ('It is for the Court, the principal judicial organ of the United Nations, to resolve any legal questions that may be in issue between parties to the dispute; and the resolution of such legal questions by the Court may be an important, and sometimes decisive, factor in promoting the peaceful settlement of the dispute'); *Military and Paramilitary Activities in and against Nicaragua* (*Nicaragua* v. *US*), 1984 ICJ at 435 (describing the functions of the Court in respect of international peace and security as 'complementary' to those of the Security Council).

18 *Application of the Convention on the Prevention and Punishment of the Crime of Genocide* (*Bosnia and Herzegovina* v. *Serbia and Montenegro*), 2007 ICJ 43, 101–102.

19 *Oil Platforms* (*Iran* v. *US*), 2003 ICJ 161, 205–207 (holding that no commerce between Iran and the US existed prior to the attack on the oil platforms, rendering moot the question of the legality of the attack) and 326–327 (Separate Opinion of Judge Simma) (calling for more extensive use of *obiter dicta* in use of force cases). See also *Legal Consequences of the Construction of a Wall in the Occupied Palestinian Territory*, 2004 ICJ 136, at 194 (holding both that self-defence does not govern military operations in occupied territories and – more controversially, and arguably, unnecessarily – that the art. 51 of the UN Charter does not cover attacks originating in non-state actors).

the Court has resorted in recent years to issuing rather bold provisional measures without a clear mandate for doing so.[20] Thus, the holdings on jurisdiction in *Military and Paramilitary Activities in Nicaragua* and in *Application of the Genocide Convention (Croatia* v. *Serbia)* may fit into a broader policy of judicial activism in the field of international peace and security.[21]

Category-based case selection by specialized courts

The role of policy considerations in determining the scope of a court's jurisdiction – that is, engaging in category-based case selection – may be particularly important in cases pending before specialized courts that operate in the context of a legal regime with a protective agenda, such as human rights courts or investment tribunals. In such cases, jurisdictional provisions are sometimes construed with an in-built mission bias, which may lead adjudicators to embrace maximalist protective positions. This could in turn translate into an expansive construction of jurisdictional mandates and a narrow reading of jurisdictional conditions.

One clear illustration of such a pro-jurisdiction bias can be found in the European Convention on Human Rights' (ECtHR's) decision on jurisdiction in *Loizidou*, where the Court reviewed the validity of a reservation appended by Turkey to its declaration accepting the Court's jurisdiction, depriving the Court of jurisdiction over violations that may have occurred outside Turkey's territory. The Court held that the effectiveness of the European Convention's system of protection could not allow such a reservation:

> If as contended by the respondent Government, substantive or territorial restrictions were permissible under these provisions, Contracting Parties would be free to subscribe to separate regimes of enforcement of Convention obligations depending on the scope of their acceptances. Such a system, which would enable States to qualify their consent under the optional clauses, would not only seriously weaken the role of the

[20] See *Request for Interpretation of the Judgment of 15 June 1962 in the Case concerning the Temple of Preah Vihear* (*Cambodia* v. *Thailand*), 2011 ICJ 537, 552–554 (provisional measures); *Application of the International Convention on the Elimination of All Forms of Racial Discrimination* (*Georgia* v. *Russian Federation*), 2008 ICJ 353, 396–397 (provisional measures).

[21] An exception to that policy trend may be found in the *Use of Force (NATO)* cases, which seem to be marked by a strong policy of judicial abstinence. See Part III.

Commission and Court in the discharge of their functions but would also diminish the effectiveness of the Convention as a constitutional instrument of European public order (*ordre public*).[22]

The fundamental importance of the Court's exercise of jurisdiction over alleged human rights violations in Europe thus created a strong presumption against the legality of a reservation, which curbed the scope of its jurisdiction, as well as against attributing to the Turkish government the intent to treat the reservation and declaration as inseparable (i.e. that the invalidity of the reservation leads to invalidity of the entire declaration of acceptance of jurisdiction).[23] Thus, unlike the ICJ in *Fisheries Jurisdiction*, the ECtHR opted in *Loizidou* for an objective, rather than subjective, interpretation of the reservation to a declaration of acceptance of jurisdiction. In both cases, however, it may arguably have been the policy on jurisdiction, and not the interpretive technique, that determined the outcome. Indeed, on other occasions the ECtHR opted for interpretations of the scope of the European Convention on the basis of the state parties' subjective views,[24] and the

[22] *Loizidou* v. *Turkey*, 1995 Eur. Ct. H.R. (ser. A) (No. 310), at para 75.

[23] *Ibid.*, at para 96 ('It thus falls to the Court, in the exercise of its responsibilities under Article 19 (art. 19), to decide this issue with reference to the texts of the respective declarations and the special character of the Convention regime. The latter, it must be said, militates in favour of the severance of the impugned clauses since it is by this technique that the rights and freedoms set out in the Convention may be ensured in all areas falling within Turkey's "jurisdiction" within the meaning of Article 1 (art. 1) of the Convention').

[24] See e.g. *Bankovic* v. *Belgium*, App. No. 52207/99, ECtHR decision of 12 December 2001, at para 62 ('The Court finds State practice in the application of the Convention since its ratification to be indicative of a lack of any apprehension on the part of the Contracting States of their extra-territorial responsibility in contexts similar to the present case. Although there have been a number of military missions involving Contracting States acting extra-territorially since their ratification of the Convention [inter alia, in the Gulf, in Bosnia and Herzegovina and in the FRY], no State has indicated a belief that its extra-territorial actions involved an exercise of jurisdiction within the meaning of Article 1 of the Convention by making a derogation pursuant to Article 15 of the Convention'); *Hassan* v. *UK*, Eur. Ct. H.R. paras 101–103 (16 September 2014) ('The practice of the High Contracting Parties is not to derogate from their obligations under Article 5 in order to detain persons on the basis of the Third and Fourth Geneva Conventions during international armed conflicts . . . In the light of the above considerations, the Court accepts the Government's argument that the lack of a formal derogation under Article 15 does not prevent the Court from taking account of the context and the provisions of international humanitarian law when interpreting and applying Article 5 in this case.').

ICJ underscored the importance of objective factors in its jurisdictional decisions.[25]

Other examples of an in-built mission bias in jurisdictional decisions may be found in the field of international investment, where investment tribunals often tend to construe the term investment broadly,[26] and to downplay the significance of objections to jurisdiction based on contractual choice of forum provisions.[27]

Of course, there may be cases in which the adjudicators in specialized courts and tribunals disagree as to what their institution's dominant policy goals should be or how they can best be advanced. One may mention in this regard the *Tokios Tokelés* case before ICSID, in which the majority and the minority disagreed on whether to accord protection to an investment made by a foreign corporation controlled by local investors. Whereas the majority was of the view that the investment protection agenda of ICSID would best be served by a refusal on the part of the tribunal to read into the relevant bilateral investment treaty (BIT) new jurisdictional conditions (excluding foreign investors controlled by local investors), the minority held the view that the same agenda would be better served by an interpretation of the foundational jurisdictional authority of ICSID tribunals in a manner that protects the investment arbitration system against abusive invocation of its dispute settlement procedures.[28]

25 See e.g. *Accordance with international law of the unilateral declaration of Independence in Respect of Kosovo*, 2010 ICJ 403, 417 ('the motives of individual States which sponsor, or vote in favour of, a resolution requesting an advisory opinion are not relevant to the Court's exercise of its discretion whether or not to respond').

26 See e.g. Nigel Blackaby *et al.*, *Guide to ICSID Arbitration*, 2nd edn. (Alphen aan den Rijn: Kluwer Law International, 2011), p. 13; *Fedax NV* v. *Venezuela*, ICSID Case No. ARB/96/3, Decision of 11 July 1997, para 25 ('the term "investment" has been broadly understood in the ICSID practice and decisions').

27 See e.g. *Compañía de Aguas del Aconquija SA and Vivendi Universasgs* v. *Argentina*, ICSID Case No. ARB/94/3, Decision on Annulment of 3 July 2002, para 101 ('where "the fundamental basis of the claim" is a treaty laying down an independent standard by which the conduct of the parties is to be judged, the existence of an exclusive jurisdiction clause in a contract between the claimant and the respondent state or one of its subdivisions cannot operate as a bar to the application of the treaty standard').

28 *Tokios Tokelés* v. *Ukraine*, ICSID Case No. ARB/02/18, Decision on Jurisdiction of 29 April 2004, at para 82 ('Were we to accept the origin of capital as transcending the textual definition of the nationality of the Claimant and the scope of covered investment in the Ukraine-Lithuania BIT, we would override the explicit choice of the Contracting Parties as to how to define these terms. Ukraine, Lithuania and

Another example of a disagreement on which policy consideration should be prioritized can be found in the decision of the Human Rights Committee in *Achabal Puertas*, where the impact of a summary resolution by the ECtHR to dismiss a parallel case on the Committee's jurisdiction was discussed. According to the majority, the Spanish *electa una via* reservation (which bars the Committee from reviewing communications already reviewed by other international complaint procedures) was only applicable where the competing process resulted in a reasoned decision suggesting a sufficient consideration of the merits of the complaint.[29] The minority view on the Committee was that the reservation should be given effect even if it is shown that only a limited consideration of merits of the complaint had been afforded by the ECtHR.[30] Here too, one may juxtapose a protectionist impulse against an attempt to give full effect to a reservation. Whereas the majority position prioritizes the victim's interest in having her complaint substantively reviewed, the minority may have sought to maintain the confidence of the state parties in the individual communication system and to limit the possibility of re-litigating before the Committee the many thousands of cases summarily dismissed by the ECtHR every year.

other Contracting Parties chose their methods of defining corporate nationality and the scope of covered investment in BITs with confidence that ICSID arbitrators would give effect to those definitions. That confidence is premised on the ICSID Convention itself, which leaves to the reasonable discretion of the parties the task of defining key terms. We should be loath to undermine it'); *Ibid.*, dissenting opinion of Mr Weil, at para 30 ('The ICSID mechanism and remedy are not meant for, and are not to be construed as, allowing – and even less encouraging – nationals of a State party to the ICSID Convention to use a foreign corporation, whether preexistent or created for that purpose, as a means of evading the jurisdiction of their domestic courts and the application of their national law. It is meant to protect – and thus encourage – international investment. It is regrettable, so it seems to me, to put the extraordinary success met by ICSID at risk by extending its scope and application beyond the limits so carefully assigned to it by the Convention').

29 HRC, *Achabal Puertas* v. *Spain*, Communication No. 1945/2010, para. 7.3, U.N. Doc. CCPR/C/107/D/1945/2010 (2013).

30 *Ibid.*, dissenting opinion of Ms Seibert-Fohr *et al.*

9

Individual case-by-case selection

Limits on discretionary interpretation of jurisdictional provisions

The exercise of some measure of discretion by international courts in construing their jurisdictional provisions is inevitable. Some of these provisions may have been deliberately drafted using ambiguous language;[1] others have become ambiguous over time due to changes in the nature of the relevant international disputes;[2] and yet other provisions are subject to conflicting interpretative techniques (e.g. the ordinary meaning of the text, its context and its object and purpose).[3] In this respect, international courts always enjoy some discretion in delineating the power delegated to them by the mandate providers, engaging thereby in incidental category-based case selection. Decisions to engage in discretionary case selection on a case-by-case basis, however, must rest on a different basis. They may be justified based on the discretion attendant to the application of jurisdictional provisions (i.e. ascertaining whether the referred dispute falls within the class of disputes which the court is authorized to adjudicate), or on the basis of the authority to exercise discretion whether to adjudicate (referred to in this book as power to determine admissibility).

[1] See e.g. Isabelle Van Damme, *Treaty Interpretation by the WTO Appellate Body* (Oxford: Oxford University Press, 2009), p. 144; Yuval Shany, 'Assessing the Effectiveness of International Courts: A Goal-Based Approach' (2012) 106 *AJIL* 225, 233.

[2] See e.g. Alexandra Huneeus, 'International Criminal Law by Other Means: The Quasi-Criminal Jurisdiction of the Human Rights Courts' (2013) 107 *AJIL* 1, 15.

[3] Vienna Convention on the Law of Treaties (VCLT), arts. 30–31.

At the same time, construing a general jurisdictional provision with the specific aim of including or excluding a particular case within its scope of coverage goes beyond what can be legitimately expected from an act of legal interpretation, which should meet requirements of consistency[4] and generality.[5] Accordingly, such conduct raises concerns of abuse of judicial discretion. The notion that similar cases should be treated alike applies to jurisdictional decisions too, and jurisdictional provisions should be assigned fixed contents that reflect some principled approach with regard to the scope of authority invested in the relevant international court. Arguably, inconsistencies in the interpretation and application of jurisdictional provisions (i.e. jurisdictional authorizations and conditions) may suggest either that a change in legal approach has taken place – which may be a natural development in the life of an international court – or, more problematically, that the judges on the panel are engaged when interpreting a general jurisdictional provision in specific case selection.

While case selection, even on a case-by-case basis, may be motivated by general and well-intentioned policy considerations, such as the need to shield an international court from embarrassing political criticism or to promote an important normative agenda (e.g. through avoiding 'bad cases' that may make 'bad law'), the advancement of such policy considerations may come at the expense of the perception that judicial decisions are predominantly governed by legal considerations. The concern is that specific case selection considerations, leading to sharp inconsistencies in the interpretation and application of the law, may exact legitimacy costs from the relevant international court since consistency is one of the main building blocks of legitimacy.[6] If I am right, then one may critically assess whether the policy considerations supporting specific case selection should have been prioritized over the need to adhere to conventional legal methods and to maintain the court's long-term legitimacy.

4 Thomas M Franck, *The Power of Legitimacy among Nations* (New York, Oxford: Oxford University Press, 1990), 142.

5 Lon Fuller, *The Morality of Law*, revised edn. (New Haven, CT: Yale University Press, 1964), p. 46.

6 See Shany, 'Assessing the Effectiveness of International Courts', p. 86.

ICJ cases involving the conflict in the Balkans

The International Court of Justice (ICJ) has a relatively stable composition (especially since resort to adjudication in chambers is quite exceptional in nature);[7] its jurisprudence tends to be predictable;[8] and its explicit powers to exercise a discretionary denial of jurisdiction are very restricted. Given the institutional pull towards consistency in decisions on jurisdiction exerted on it, the ICJ serves as an interesting case study for the proposition that jurisdictional decisions may sometimes serve the purposes of specific case selection. Specifically, the series of ICJ cases, involving questions of jurisdiction over the state of Yugoslavia during the period 1995–2015, may serve as prime examples of inconsistent law interpretation and application, suggesting resort by the Court to specific case selection in the course of the exercise of its interpretive powers.

In its 2004 judgments on the cases brought by Yugoslavia against several NATO member states, the Court held that Yugoslavia's decision to seek readmission to the United Nations (UN) in 2000 implied that it was not a member in 1999 when it initiated court proceedings.[9] Thus, the Court lacked foundational jurisdiction *ratione personae* over the applicant state. The 2004 judgments, which were based on a very narrow – and to my mind rather questionable – interpretation of article 35(2) of the ICI Statute,[10] threw into doubt the status of two previous decisions issued in the *Application of the Genocide Convention* (*Bosnia* v. *Serbia*) case – the 1993 provisional measures decision and the 1996 judgment on preliminary objections – and the outcome of the proceedings initiated against Serbia by Croatia. In these other cases, the Court's authority to adjudicate was premised on the belief that Yugoslavia was a state and that the ICJ consequently had jurisdiction *ratione personae* over it. Since nothing in the text of article 35 of the Statute distinguishes between the foundational jurisdiction of the Court over applicants and

[7] Paolo Palchetti, 'Article 26', in Andreas Zimmermann *et al.* (eds.), *The Statute of the International Court of Justice: A Commentary*, 2nd edn. (Oxford: Oxford University Press, 2012), pp. 500–501.

[8] Anthony Aust, *Handbook of International Law*, 2nd edn. (Cambridge: Cambridge University Press, 2010), p. 413.

[9] *Legality of Use of Force* (*Serbia and Montenegro* v. *Belgium*), 2004 ICJ 279, 310–311.

[10] *Ibid.*, 324.

respondents,[11] it stands to reason that if Yugoslavia was not a member between its dissolution in 1991–1992 and its readmission to the UN in 2000, then Bosnia was not entitled to initiate proceedings against it in 1993 and Croatia did not have the right to bring a case against it in 1999.

The Court used three controversial interpretive moves in order to reach the counter-intuitive result according to which Yugoslavia had no access to the Court as an applicant but could nonetheless be sued before it. First, in its 2007 *Application of the Genocide Convention* (*Bosnia* v. *Serbia*), the Court applied the *res judicata* principle in an extremely broad manner, conferring *res judicata* status on a judgment issued in a previous stage of the same case – the 1996 judgment on preliminary objections.[12] It did so despite persistent doubts as to whether this principle even applies to jurisdictional decisions (in the light of past *dicta* by the Court questioning the *res judicata* status of judgments on jurisdiction),[13] as to whether the *res judicata* principle may overcome the lack of foundational jurisdiction[14] and as to whether the issue of Yugoslavia's UN membership was seriously considered by the 1996 judgment in a manner to which a *res judicata* effect can attach.[15]

[11] ICJ Statute, art. 35 reads:

> 1. The Court shall be open to the states parties to the present Statute; 2. The conditions under which the Court shall be open to other states shall, subject to the special provisions contained in treaties in force, be laid down by the Security Council, but in no case shall such conditions place the parties in a position of inequality before the Court.; 3. When a state which is not a Member of the United Nations is a party to a case, the Court shall fix the amount which that party is to contribute towards the expenses of the Court. This provision shall not apply if such state is bearing a share of the expenses of the Court.

[12] *Application of the Convention on the Prevention and Punishment of the Crime of Genocide* (*Bosnia and Herzegovina* v. *Serbia and Montenegro*), 2007 ICJ 43, 101–102.

[13] *South West Africa* (*Ethiopia* v. *South Africa*), 1966 ICJ 6, 36:

> As regards the issue of preclusion, the Court finds it unnecessary to pronounce on various issues which have been raised in this connection, such as whether a decision on a preliminary objection constitutes a res judicata in the proper sense of that term, – whether it ranks as a "decision" for the purposes of Article 59 of the Court's Statute, or as "final" within the meaning of Article 60.

[14] *Application of the Convention on the Prevention and Punishment of the Crime of Genocide* (*Bosnia and Herzegovina* v. *Serbia and Montenegro*), 2007 ICJ 43, 100–101 (discussing Serbia's claims against the assignment of *res judicata* to the 1996 judgment).

[15] *Ibid.*, at 96–99 (discussing Serbia's argument that the question of access to the court was not adequately discussed in the 2006 judgment).

Second, the Court applied its powers of revision in a restrictive manner, refusing to invoke its power to open proceedings due to discovery of new facts. In both the 2003 judgment on the *Application for Revision of the 1996 Judgment in Application of the Genocide Convention* (*Bosnia* v. *Serbia*) and in the 2007 judgment on the merits of the same case, the Court held that the power of legal revision only covers the discovery of a fact which already existed at the time the judgment was issued.[16] By qualifying Serbia's 2000 admission to the UN as a 'new fact' and not as a new development leading to the discovery of an 'old fact' (the status of membership in 1993), the Court opted for a narrow interpretation of its power of revision under article 61 of the Statute. In the circumstances of the case, this interpretative move created a legal straightjacket preventing the Court from considering a dramatic development in a case still pending before it: the clarification of Serbia's UN membership status throughout the 1990s. It thus refused to consider the claim that the 2000 admission implied that Serbia was not a UN member in 1993 when the case was launched, and, as a result, that the factual premise on which the Court based its foundational jurisdiction *ratione personae* had collapsed.[17]

Finally, in the *Application of the Genocide Convention* (*Croatia* v. *Serbia*) judgment on preliminary objections, the Court applied the *Mavrommatis* doctrine allowing it to ignore curable flaws in jurisdiction at the moment of seisin, when such flaws may have been remedied by subsequent events, which would permit the resubmission of the case to the Court.[18] However, it is not fully clear whether this doctrine, which is based on 'sound administration of justice' considerations, is suitable for fixing flaws in the Court's foundational jurisdiction (such as right of access to the Court).[19] Nor is it fully clear

[16] *Ibid.*, 88–89; *Application for Revision of the Judgment of 11 July 1996 in the Case concerning Application of the Convention on the Prevention and Punishment of the Crime of Genocide* (*Bosnia and Herzegovina* v. *Yugoslavia*), 2003 ICJ 7, 30–31 (Preliminary Objections).

[17] Stephen Wittich, 'Permissible Derogation from Mandatory Rules? The Problem of Party Status in the Genocide Case' (2007) 18 *EJIL* 595.

[18] *Application of the Convention on the Prevention and Punishment of the Crime of Genocide* (*Croatia* v. *Serbia*), 2008 ICJ 412, 441.

[19] *Ibid.*, 475 (Joint Declaration of judges Ranjeva, Shi, Koroma, and Parra-Aranguren) ('For the Court to conclude, on the basis of this *obiter dictum* in the *Mavrommatis* case, that the Respondent has access to it and it has jurisdiction over the Respondent is a misapplication of the Permanent Court's comment. The present case does not lend itself to the approach taken in *Mavrommatis*, because the *Mavrommatis* case did not concern access').

why the application of the *Mavrommatis* doctrine was not considered *proprio motu* in the *Use of Force (NATO)* judgments (one possible reason why Yugoslavia did not rely on the doctrine in it would have harmed its litigation interests in the cases brought against it by Bosnia and Herzegovina and Croatia).[20] Furthermore, by 2008, when the preliminary objections in the case were decided, it seems as if Croatia could no longer bring a case against Serbia – because of the latter's 2001 reservation to the Genocide Convention excluding the jurisdiction of the Court over genocide claims.[21] Hence, it appears as if the application of the *Mavrommatis* doctrine by the Court was of an extremely loose nature (allowing for resubmission of the application if at any specific point in time between the initial application and the judgment conditions for jurisdiction were met), if not outright erroneous.[22]

These legal acrobatics by the Court, oscillating between extremes of legal formalism and disdain for form, have been strongly criticized by some members of the Court. In their joint dissent in *Application of the Genocide Convention (Bosnia* v. *Serbia)*, judges Shi, Rajeva and Koroma were of the view that 'judicial consistency would have required the Court to respond as it did in the Legality of Use of Force cases'.[23]

[20] *Ibid.*, 442–443:

> It is true that the Court apparently did not take account in its 2004 Judgments of the fact that Serbia and Montenegro had by that date become a party to the Statute . . . But if the Court abided in those cases strictly by the general rule that its jurisdiction is to be assessed at the date of filing of the act instituting proceedings, without adopting the more flexible approach following from the other decisions cited above, that is justified by particular considerations relevant to those cases. It was clear that Serbia and Montenegro did not have the intention of pursuing its claims by way of new applications.

[21] Reservation by Yugoslavia to the Convention on the Prevention and Punishment of the Crime of Genocide, 12 March 2001:

> The Federal Republic of Yugoslavia does not consider itself bound by Article IX of the Convention on the Prevention and Punishment of the Crime of Genocide and, therefore, before any dispute to which the Federal Republic of Yugoslavia is a party may be validly submitted to the jurisdiction of the International Court of Justice under this Article, the specific and explicit consent of the FRY is required in each case.

[22] *Application of the Convention on the Prevention and Punishment of the Crime of Genocide* (*Croatia* v. *Serbia*), 2008 ICJ at 470 (Separate Opinion of Vice-President Al-Khasawneh).

[23] *Application of the Convention on the Prevention and Punishment of the Crime of Genocide* (*Bosnia and Herzegovina* v. *Serbia and Montenegro*), 2007 ICJ 43, 274 (Joint Dissenting Opinion of judges Ranjeva, Shi and Koroma).

Furthermore, Judge Al-Khasawneh (who also objected to the holding in the *Use of Force (NATO)* cases) noted in his dissent to the 2007 *Application of the Genocide Convention (Bosnia* v. *Serbia)* judgment that the 2004 judgments had a 'negative and regrettable impact on the broad consistency of the Court's jurisprudence'.[24] In the same vein, in his separate opinion in the 2008 *Application of the Genocide Convention (Croatia* v. *Serbia)* judgment, Judge Al-Khasawneh criticized the Court's decision to deviate from the 2004 judgments, notwithstanding the fact that it was finally 'freed from the shackles of res judicata', since the parties to the 1996 and 2008 judgments were different.[25]

Arguably, the fluctuations in this series of decisions may be explained by specific case-selection considerations. It can be speculated that the Court was reluctant to exercise jurisdiction over the *Use of Force (NATO)* cases because it did not want to confront a group of powerful states, who strongly objected to the subjection of their military operations in Yugoslavia to judicial review.[26] It is also possible that the Court had little appetite for addressing the controversial question of the legality of humanitarian intervention under international law raised by some of the *Use of Force (NATO)* cases.[27] At the same time, it seems as if the Court went out of its way to retain jurisdiction over the two genocide cases lodged by Bosnia and Croatia against Yugoslavia. One may hypothesize that this judicial policy choice was related to the institutional interest of the Court of establishing itself as a relevant forum for international peace and security cases[28] (which do not unduly embarrass certain

[24] *Ibid.*, at 249 (Dissenting Opinion of Vice-President Al-Khasawneh).

[25] *Application of the Convention on the Prevention and Punishment of the Crime of Genocide* (*Croatia* v. *Serbia*), 2008 ICJ at 469 (Separate Opinion of Vice-President Al-Khasawneh).

[26] It may be speculated that similar reluctance to confront NATO member states led the European Court of Human Rights (ECtHR) to deny jurisdiction in the *Bankovic* case, and the International Criminal Tribunal for Yugoslavia (ICTY) Office of the Prosecutor to refrain from recommending a criminal investigation into alleged NATO war crimes. Final Report to the Prosecutor by the Committee Established to Review the NATO Bombing Campaign against the Federal Republic of Yugoslavia, published on 13 June 2000, www.icty.org/sid/10052.

[27] Arguably, a similar impulse to avoid deeply controversial legal questions may also explain the extremely narrow approach taken by the Court in responding to the request for an advisory opinion in *Accordance with International Law of the Unilateral Declaration of Independence in Respect of Kosovo*, 2010 ICJ 403.

[28] An expression of this institutional interest can be found in Judge Simma's *dicta* in the *Oil Platforms* case. *Oil Platforms* (*Iran* v. *US*), 2003 ICJ 161, 327

powerful states or groups of states). Another possible explanation for the Court's interest in assuming jurisdiction over the genocide cases may be the adoption of a victim-oriented attitude by some of the Court's judges – an attitude of construing international norms, including jurisdictional norms, in a manner that is consistent with the need to protect individual victims.[29]

Indeed, it is quite possible that the Court's reputation would have suffered some harm had it reached the opposite outcomes than the ones it reached: declining jurisdiction over claims charging a state with genocidal policies, while accepting jurisdiction to review the operations of states that intervened in order to stop the perpetration of further atrocities. To the extent that the Court is concerned with building and maintaining its institutional legitimacy, one may contend that considerations of generating just outcomes – condemning international crimes (which may be regarded as 'outcome legitimacy' considerations)[30] – might have trumped considerations related to the Court's need to adhere to its jurisdictional mandate and to treat all cases alike (which may be regarded as 'source and process legitimacy' considerations).[31]

To the extent that the Court is concerned about the effectiveness of its work (goal attainment),[32] the outcomes reached in the two genocide cases can also be supported by way of reference to the ICJ's norm-supporting mission.[33] As indicated earlier in this chapter, one may claim that the international law interpreting, applying and developing role of the Court is well served whenever it exercises jurisdiction over a dispute-raising question of great legal importance. Such normative influence may, however, be partly offset by the loss of legitimacy in the eyes of some potential parties, who may be less inclined to utilize the Court or follow its decisions as a result of their legally controversial jurisdictional basis.

(Separate Opinion of Judge Simma) ('I consider it of utmost importance, and a matter of principle, for the Court to pronounce itself on questions of the threat or use of force in international relations whenever it is given the opportunity to do so').

[29] See e.g., Antonio A Cançado Trindade, *The Construction of a Humanized International Law* (Leiden: Martinus Nijhoff Publishers, 2014), p. 84 (a reprint of Judge Cançado's Separate Opinion in *La Cantuta* v. *Peru*, Inter American Court of Human Rights, Interpretation of Judgment 30 November 2007).

[30] See Shany, 'Assessing the Effectiveness of International Courts', pp. 143–145.

[31] *Ibid.*, 141–142. [32] *Ibid.*, 6–8. [33] *Ibid.*, 38–40.

Other possible instances of specific case selection in ICJ decisions

The tension between the need to maintain legal consistency in construing jurisdictional provisions and policy considerations pointing in other directions may have manifested itself in other sets of ICJ cases in which the Court appears to have deviated from its past jurisprudence on jurisdictional matters without a compelling doctrinal reason. Among such sets, one may mention the series of ICJ cases on the question of whether letters, communiqués or minutes suggesting an intent to refer a case to the ICJ in the future, if negotiations fail, constitute a valid form of consent to jurisdiction;[34] whether instruments expressing consent to the jurisdiction of the Permanent Court of International Justice (PCIJ) can be relied upon to establish the jurisdiction of the ICJ in circumstances where a party to the PCIJ Statute was not an original UN member;[35] and how to determine the date on which a dispute has arisen for jurisdictional purposes in situations of a legal conflict comprising several stages or incidents.[36]

To be sure, most if not all of these in consistencies can be explained away through reference to minor differences in the facts of the case or the language of the legal instruments relied upon to establish jurisdiction.[37] Still, it may be speculated that policy considerations

[34] See *Aegean Sea Continental Shelf* (*Greece* v. *Turkey*), 1978 ICJ 3, 43–44; *Application of the Convention on the Prevention and Punishment of the Crime of Genocide* (*Bosnia and Herzegovina* v. *Yugoslavia*), 1996 ICJ 595, 618 (preliminary objections); *Maritime Delimitation and Territorial Questions* (*Qatar* v. *Bahrain*), 1994 ICJ 112, 120–122 (jurisdiction and admissibility I).

[35] See *Aerial Incident of 27 July 1955*, 1959 ICJ 127, 136–142; *Barcelona Traction, Light and Power Company, Ltd* (*Belgium* v. *Spain*), 1964 ICJ 6, 29–35 (preliminary objections).

[36] See *Legality of Use of Force* (*Yugoslavia* v. *Belgium*), 1999 ICJ 124, 134–135 (provisional measures); *Certain Property* (*Liechtenstein* v. *Germany*), 2005 ICJ 6, 25–27; *Right of Passage over Indian Territory* (*Portugal* v. *India*), 1960 ICJ 6, 33–35.

[37] E.g., in *Barcelona Traction*, the Court distinguished between the expiration of optional clause declarations at the demise of the PCIJ Statute and the continued validity of treaty provisions referring disputes to the PCIJ in the following terms:

> Not only is a different category of instrument involved – an instrument having a conventional form, not that of a unilateral declaration – but the essential requirement of being "in force", which in the cases contemplated by Article 36, paragraph 5, bore directly on the jurisdictional clause–the unilateral declaration itself–is, in Article 37, formally related not to the clause as such, but to the instrument–the treaty or convention–containing it.

relating to the Court's institutional interests – in particular, its legitimacy and effectiveness – may have encouraged the Court to emphasize the differences between the said cases and to *de facto* engage in specific case selection.[38] Thus, it is possible that in the *Use of Force (NATO)* (provisional measures) the Court gave an objective meaning to Yugoslavia's temporal reservation (notwithstanding its clear intent to confer upon the Court jurisdiction to review NATO's attacks against it), in deviation from its holding in *Fisheries Jurisdiction* that such reservations should be read in the light of the subjective intent of the reserving party,[39] partly because such review could complicate the ongoing humanitarian intervention operation and put the Court in the awkward position of ordering the ceasing of efforts to protect the civilian population of Kosovo against Serbian violence. It is also possible that the difference in the manner of treatment of declarations of acceptance of jurisdiction between the 1959 *Aerial Incident* case and the 1984 *Military and Paramilitary Activities in Nicaragua* case[40] are related

Barcelona Traction, Light and Power Company, Ltd (*Belgium* v. *Spain*), 1964 ICJ 6, 29. But see *ibid.*, 48 (Declaration of Judge Spiropoulos) ('my position is determined by the Court's Judgment in the case concerning the Aerial Incident [*Israel* v. *Bulgaria*]. Starting from the concept that the purpose of Article 37 of the Statute of the Court is the same as that of Article 36, paragraph 5, and basing myself on the considerations of the Judgment in question, I consider that the Court should have found that it is without jurisdiction').

38 For an implicit admission of the role of policy consideration in differently construing two comparable jurisdictional clauses, see *ibid.*, at 29–30:

> Nor can the Court be oblivious to other differences which cannot but affect the question of the need for the Court to make an independent approach to the present case ... [A]ny decision of the Court, relative to Article 37, must affect a considerable number of surviving treaties and conventions providing for recourse to the Permanent Court, including instruments of a political or technical character, and certain general multilateral conventions of great importance that seem likely to continue in force. It is thus clear that the decision of the Court in the present case, whatever it might be, would be liable to have far-reaching effects. This is in no way a factor which should be allowed to influence the legal character of that decision: but it does constitute a reason why the decision should not be regarded as already predetermined by that which was given in the different circumstances of the Israel *v.* Bulgaria case.

39 *Fisheries Jurisdiction* (*Spain* v. *Canada*), 1998 ICJ 432, 454.

40 In *Aerial Incident*, the Court held that the Bulgarian declaration of acceptance of jurisdiction expired with the demise of the PCIJ in 1946, and was not revived upon the accession of Bulgaria to the ICJ in 1955. 1959 ICJ 127. In *Military and Paramilitary Activities in Nicaragua*, the Court held that Nicaragua's 1929 declaration of acceptance of PCIJ jurisdiction could be relied upon following its accession to the ICJ and its inclusion in official publications of 'optional

to the Court's interest to extricate itself from Cold War related issues in the 1950s and to regain the confidence of the developing world in the 1980s by serving as a forum for challenging the policies of one of the global superpowers.

Finally, it might be hypothesized that the Court's willingness to be more flexible in identifying consent to its jurisdiction in *Maritime Delimitation Qatar-Bahrain* than in earlier cases is related to the Court's interest in extending the geographical reach of its jurisprudence to the Arab world. It may also be the case that a majority of the Court's judges assumed that Bahrain would eventually agree to participate in the proceedings, and were thus willing to downplay the significance of some of the formal deficiencies of the contingent form in which consent to jurisdiction was expressed.[41] While I do not have any empirical proof that policy considerations of this nature led to specific case selection in these and other cases, it looks as if the applicable jurisdictional rules were open-ended enough in nature so as to facilitate the weighing of such policy considerations in the course of their interpretation or application, had the Court wished to weigh them.

Just to be clear, there is nothing inherently problematic with a case-by-case approach to the exercise of jurisdiction. In domestic legal systems, superior courts often enjoy discretion on whether to exercise jurisdiction (a notable example being the discretionary grant of *certiorari* by the United States Supreme Court),[42] and as the next part of this book shows, several international courts have

clause states', although the dilation never entered into force for the PCIJ. 1984 ICJ 392 (Jurisdiction of the Court and Admissibility of the Application).

41 One mark of the unease felt by ICJ judges in accepting jurisdiction based on indefinite meeting minutes has been the exceptional opportunity afforded to the parties to reach an agreement which clarifies the scope of the issues to be referred to the ICJ before discussion of the merits. *Maritime Delimitation and Territorial Questions* (*Qatar* v. *Bahrain*), 1994 ICJ 112, 125 ('The Court has consequently decided to afford the Parties the opportunity to ensure the submission to the Court of the entire dispute as it is comprehended within the 1990 Minutes and the Bahraini formula, to which they have both agreed'). The halfway position adopted by the Court does not sit well with past *dicta* on the need to establish consent to jurisdiction by an unconditional and immediate commitment, and it encountered some criticism from judges that submitted individual opinions. See e.g., *ibid.*, 130–131 (separate opinion of Vice-President Schwebel); *ibid.*, 132 (separate opinion of Judge Valticos); *ibid.*, 134–135 (dissenting opinion of Judge Oda).

42 The Judiciary Act of 1891, 26 Stat. 826, codified as amended at 28 USC § 43 (2006).

discretionary powers to dismiss claims as inadmissible. Nevertheless, the engagement in specific case selection without explicit authorization in the constitutive instruments of the international court in question runs the risk of appearing to treat like cases differently and to construe the court's powers in a tendentious manner. Such perceptions of selectivity in law interpretation and law application undermine the myth of international courts as institutions governed by objective principles, applying predetermined general norms and operating separately from international politics (that may recommend a case-by-case approach to international conflicts) and free from political pressures. Ultimately, selective application of jurisdictional provisions may detract from the legitimacy of international courts and erode respect for the rule of law in international relations.

Accordingly, international courts might find themselves caught between two conflicting sets of values and interests. On the one hand, the uniform application of their jurisdictional provisions would conform to acceptable legal practices and increase the legitimacy of international courts in the eyes of some constituencies. On the other hand, without the ability to engage in specific case selection international courts may be deprived of an important tool, which could increase their prospects of advancing judicial policies that may help them garner support from other constituencies. For example, if the jurisdictional straightjacket in which the Court operates prevents it from denouncing genocide, its effectiveness as a norm-supporting and dispute-resolving institution may be reduced. Put differently, strict adherence to consistent interpretation and application of jurisdictional provisions support the Court's image as an agent or trustee operating on behalf of its two principal constituencies – the mandate providers and the parties to the case. At the same time, however, case selection remains an important method by which the goals of these mandate providers – that is, judicial effectiveness – can be advanced or prioritized.

Part III

Questions of admissibility before international courts

10

The taxonomical challenge

Distinguishing jurisdiction from admissibility

This part is dedicated to review of questions of admissibility. I will first address the taxonomical challenge confronting international lawyers discussing admissibility. Generally speaking, the literature on the jurisdiction of international courts often struggles to distinguish questions of admissibility from ones of jurisdiction.[1] The case law on the matter has also sometimes been less than clear, and at times the very need for offering a distinction between the two concepts has been questioned. In *Mavrommatis*, for example, the Permanent Court of International Justice (PCIJ) already noted that the Court 'need not consider whether "competence" and "jurisdiction", incompetence and *fin de non-recevoir* should invariably and in every connection be regarded as synonymous expressions'.[2] The different provisions

[1] See e.g., Andrew P Newcombe and Lluís Paradell, *Law and Practice of Investment Treaties: Standards of Treatment* (Alphen aan den Rijn: Kluwer Law International, 2009), p. 221 ('the distinction between admissibility and jurisdiction is very difficult to apply'); Luiz Eduardo Salles, *Forum Shopping in International Adjudication: The Role of Preliminary Objections* (Cambridge: Cambridge University Press, 2014), p. 178 ('The line between jurisdiction and admissibility may be difficult to draw or may not really matter in all cases'); Chittharanjan F Amerasinghe, *International Arbitral Jurisdiction* (Leiden: Martinus Nijhoff Publishers, 2011), p. 71; SI Strong, 'Limits of Autonomy in International Investment Arbitration: Are Contractual Waivers of Mass Procedures Available', in Arthur W. Rovine (ed.), *Contemporary Issues in International Arbitration and Mediation: The Fordham Papers 2013* (Leiden: Martinus Nijhoff Publishers, 2014), p. 176.

[2] See *Mavrommatis Palestine Concession* (*Greece* v. *GB*), 1924 PCIJ (ser A), No. 2, at 10. Also see *Nuclear Tests* (*Australia* v. *France*), 1974 ICJ 253, 363 (dissenting opinion of Judges Onekama *et al.*):

found in the constitutive instruments of distinct international courts that sometime use different labels for the same conditions further contribute to this taxonomical confusion, as they apply these labels inconsistently and, at times, interchangeably.[3]

Still, the distinction between jurisdiction and admissibility (or between analogous concepts alluding to authority to adjudicate and power to refrain from exercising adjudicative authority) can play a useful role in practical terms and for analytical reasons. In practical terms, the distinction may help the logical sequencing of the procedure from binary questions of authority to often more complex questions of propriety, in allocating the burdens of proof between the parties, and in delineating the *proprio motu* responsibility of the relevant international court with regard to the exercise of its adjudicative powers. In analytical terms, this distinction may help us better understand the way courts exercise judicial power and the legal interests of relevant constituencies affected as they do so.

One common denominator of many past attempts to distinguish questions of jurisdiction from questions of admissibility has been the notion that the former category addresses more fundamental issues than the latter.[4] Hence, for example, Amerasinghe suggests

> it would be pointless for us to characterize any particular issue as one of jurisdiction or of admissibility, more especially as the practice neither of the Permanent Court nor of this Court supports the drawing of a sharp distinction between preliminary objections to jurisdiction and admissibility. In the Court's practice the emphasis has been laid on the essentially preliminary or non-preliminary character of the particular objection rather than on its classification as a matter of jurisdiction or admissibility.

[3] See e.g., ICJ Rules, Rule 79 (using both terms without distinguishing between them); ECHR, arts. 32, 35 (listing under jurisdiction only jurisdiction *ratione materiae* – 'matters concerning the interpretation and application of the Convention and the Protocols', and under admissibility – exhaustion of local remedies, the six months rule, anonymity, *electa una via* (fork in the road), incompatibility with the convention, manifest ill-foundedness, abuse of right, and *de minimis*); ICC Statute, arts. 12, 13, 17 (referring to issues of nature of crime, nationality of the accused, territory in which the crime occurred and triggering mechanisms as issues of jurisdiction, and to complementarity, *ne bis in idem* and gravity as matter of admissibility); Optional Protocol to the ICCPR, arts. 1–3, 5 (implying that the identity of the parties and the allusion to a violation of Covenant rights are matters of 'competence' and that anonymity, incompatibility with the Covenant and abuse of rights are matters of admissibility. No categorization is offered for other conditions – exhaustion of remedies and *lis alibi pendens*).

[4] See e.g., Robert Kolb, *The International Court of Justice* (Oxford: Hart Publishing Ltd, 2014), p. 202; William W Burke-White and Scott Kaplan, 'Shaping the Contours of

that, unlike jurisdictional deficiencies, problems of inadmissibility or irreceivability are typically curable and can be waived by the parties.[5] Fitzmaurice has claimed that questions of jurisdiction must be viewed as more fundamental than those of admissibility, as the competence of an international court to consider objections of the latter kind depends on it establishing its jurisdiction to begin with.[6] Consequently, it has been argued that the distinction implies not only certain procedural implications (such as the order of examining preliminary objections and allocation of burdens of proof), but also a qualitative difference between jurisdiction and admissibility.

My approach to the distinction between jurisdiction and admissibility, which I elaborate later in this chapter, focuses on the difference between power to adjudicate and power not to exercise the power to adjudicate. Though articulated in rather abstract terms, it does not differ significantly in practical terms from the position expressed by Judge Fitzmaurice in his separate opinion in *Northern Cameroons* on the difference between jurisdiction and *receivability*:

> [T]he real distinction and test would seem to be whether or not the objection is based on, or arises from, the jurisdictional clause or clauses under which the jurisdiction of the tribunal is said to exist. If so, the objection is basically one of jurisdiction. If it is founded on considerations lying outside the ambit of any jurisdictional clause, and not involving the interpretation or application of such a provision, then it will normally be an objection to the receivability of the claim.[7]

Domestic Justice: The International Criminal Court and the Admissibility Challenge in the Uganda Situation', in Carsten Stahn and Göran Sluiter (eds.), *The Emerging Practice of the International Criminal Court* (Leiden: Martinus Nijhoff Publishers, 2009), p. 98; Chittharanjan F Amerasinghe, *Jurisdiction of International Tribunals* (The Hague: Kluwer Law International, 2003), p. 71.

5 Amerasinghe, *International Arbitral Jurisdiction*, p. 71. It seems as if Amerasinghe distinguishes in effect between foundational jurisdiction, which defines the international court's overall powers (and is indeed fundamental in nature in the sense that it is located beyond the control of the parties to the case), and specific jurisdiction, which appertains to the authority bestowed on the international court by the parties.

6 Gerald Fitzmaurice, 'The Law and Procedure of the International Court of Justice, 1951–4: Questions of Jurisdiction, Competence and Procedure' (1958) 34 Brit. Y.B. Int'l L., 12–13. See also Hugh Thirlway, 'The Law and Procedure of International Courts and Tribunals, 1960–1989 – Supplement 2010: Parts Nine and Ten' (2011) 81 Brit. Y.B. Int'l L. 13, 140–141.

7 *Northern Cameroons* (*Cameroon* v. *United Kingdom*), 1963 ICJ 15, 101 (separate opinion of Judge Fitzmaurice).

As Thirlway shows, the International Court of Justice (ICJ) has in several recent cases adopted a distinction between jurisdiction and admissibility based on the connection underscored by Judge Fitzmaurice between the objection and the relevant jurisdictional clause.[8] For instance, in *Armed Activities in Congo* the Court held that:

> When that consent is expressed in a compromissory clause in an international agreement, any conditions to which such consent is subject must be regarded as constituting the limits thereon. The Court accordingly considers that the examination of such conditions relates to its jurisdiction and not to the admissibility of the application.[9]

Questions related to the interpretation and application of the jurisdictional clause or clauses touch on the international court's power to decide a dispute or apply law to a certain factual situation. And questions relating to considerations other than the scope and application of the jurisdictional clause or clauses do not challenge its legal authority to adjudicate, but rather examine whether it is proper for the court to adjudicate. In other words, questions of admissibility presume the existence of jurisdiction, but investigate whether there are valid reasons that should lead an international court to decline to exercise the power it has been entrusted with.[10]

Before elaborating on what may constitute valid reasons to decline jurisdiction, it is useful to note that the distinction between jurisdiction and admissibility is just one of several relevant distinctions relating to the exercise of the power to adjudicate, including foundational jurisdiction versus specific jurisdiction, jurisdictional authorizations versus jurisdictional conditions, and jurisdictional questions versus issues of substance of a preliminary nature. Some of the features which have been attributed in the literature to the

[8] Thirlway, 'The Law and Procedure of International Courts and Tribunals', 141–144.

[9] *Armed Activities on the Territory of the Congo* (*DRC* v. *Rwanda*), 2006 ICJ 6, 39. See also *Certain Questions of Mutual Assistance in Criminal Matters* (*Djibouti* v. *France*) 2008 ICJ 177, 200–201.

[10] *Application of the Convention on the Prevention and Punishment of the Crime of Genocide* (*Croatia* v. *Serbia*), 2008 ICJ 412, 456 ('A preliminary objection to admissibility covers a more disparate range of possibilities… Essentially such an objection consists in the contention that there exists a legal reason, even when there is jurisdiction, why the Court should decline to hear the case, or more usually, a specific claim therein').

distinction between jurisdiction and admissibility, such as curability, fundamental nature and the order in which objections are to be disposed, also appertain to other jurisdiction-related distinctions and thus are not always helpful. For instance, flaws in specific jurisdiction may also be cured through party consent,[11] and some foundational jurisdictional conditions (such as minimal or maximal waiting periods before initiation of proceedings) do not appear to be of a fundamental substantive importance, yet failure to comply with them may strip the relevant international court of jurisdiction.[12] Furthermore, the ability of international courts to dispose of cases based on preliminary questions of substance even before jurisdiction has been firmly established casts doubts on the significance of the order in which international courts review preliminary objections.[13] Put in this light, the distinction between jurisdiction and admissibility may be regarded as one of several possible distinctions pertaining to the power to adjudicate that may have a practical or analytical value. Moreover, the dividing lines delineating all of these distinctions are often blurred, leading to differences of opinion on how to classify specific preliminary objections.

Application of the distinction to jurisdictional conditions

As noted earlier, Judge Fitzmaurice proposed a distinction between jurisdiction and admissibility objections based on their reliance on the jurisdictional clause or clauses or on other considerations lying

[11] See e.g., *Certain Questions of Mutual Assistance in Criminal Matters* (*Djibouti* v. *France*) 2008 ICJ 177, 203–204 (allowing a case initially brought without the consent of the respondent state to proceed on the basis of the *forum prorogatum* doctrine). The ICJ was also of the controversial view that even flaws in foundational jurisdiction may be cured by subsequent events. *Application of the Convention on the Prevention and Punishment of the Crime of Genocide* (*Croatia* v. *Serbia*), 2008 ICJ 412, 442 ('the Court cannot accept Serbia's argument that when the defect is that one party does not have access to the Court, it is so fatal that it can in no case be cured by a subsequent event in the course of the proceedings').

[12] See e.g., *Application of the International Convention on the Elimination of All Forms of Racial Discrimination* (*Georgia* v. *Russian Federation*), 2011 ICJ 70, 140 (holding that the absence of prior negotiations – a precondition to the exercise of jurisdiction – results in an inability to found jurisdiction upon the CERD).

[13] See e.g., *Anglo-Iranian Oil* (*UK* v. *Iran*), 1952 ICJ 93, 112 (holding during review of preliminary objections that Iran did not undertake obligations towards the UK, but rather towards a UK firm).

outside the clause's ambit. Presented with the theoretical terms introduced in earlier chapters, one can understand Fitzmaurice's distinction as involving questions relating, on the one hand, to the interpretation and application of the adjudicative powers conferred on an international court by its mandate providers and by the parties, and on the other hand to other considerations that may explain why existing jurisdiction should not be exercised.

The point of departure for discussing the notion of such 'other considerations' – that is, questions of admissibility – is as follows: Without proper legal authorization, international courts cannot exceed the adjudicative powers conferred upon them explicitly or implicitly by their mandate providers and the disputing parties. In the same vein, they cannot refuse without proper authorization to exercise the adjudicative powers. Otherwise, the disputing parties might lose the right of access to an international court in order to uphold their rights and interests.[14]

Still, there may be exceptional circumstances in which a court may be justified in deciding not to exercise the power to adjudicate, which the parties validly conferred upon it.[15] These exceptional

[14] See e.g., *Mexico – Tax Measures on Soft Drinks and Other Beverages*, Report of the AB of 6 March 2006, WTO Doc. WT/DS308/AB/R, paras 51–53

> Under Article 11 of the DSU, a panel is, therefore, charged with the obligation to "make an objective assessment of the matter before it, including an objective assessment of the facts of the case and the applicability of and conformity with the relevant covered agreements." Article 11 also requires that a panel "make such other findings as will assist the DSB in making the recommendations or in giving the rulings provided for in the covered agreements." It is difficult to see how a panel would fulfil that obligation if it declined to exercise validly established jurisdiction and abstained from making any finding on the matter before it ... The fact that a Member may initiate a WTO dispute whenever it considers that "any benefits accruing to [that Member] are being impaired by measures taken by another Member" implies that that Member is entitled to a ruling by a WTO panel. A decision by a panel to decline to exercise validly established jurisdiction would seem to "diminish" the right of a complaining Member to "seek the redress of a violation of obligations" within the meaning of Article 23 of the DSU, and to bring a dispute pursuant to Article 3.3 of the DSU. This would not be consistent with a panel's obligations under Articles 3.2 and 19.2 of the DSU.1.

[15] See e.g., *Northern Cameroons* (*Cameroon* v. *UK*),1963 ICJ 15, 29 ('[E]ven if the Court, when seised, finds that it has jurisdiction, the Court is not compelled in every case to exercise that jurisdiction'); *Nottebohm* (*Liechtenstein* v. *Guatemala*), 1953 ICJ 111, 122 (the Court must exercise its powers under the Statute 'whenever it has been regularly seised and whenever it has not been shown, on some other ground, that it lacks jurisdiction or that the claim is inadmissible').

circumstances may be captured by the term 'inadmissibility' or 'irreceivability'. They differ from many, if not most, of the conditions that are found in the constitutive instruments of international courts and other jurisdiction-conferring instruments that delineate the jurisdiction of international courts. These latter conditions, which govern the exercise of jurisdiction, should be viewed as jurisdictional in nature and not issues of admissibility, regardless of the formal designation attached to them in the literature or in the constitutive instrument itself. The reason for this is that they regulate the authority to adjudicate that was delegated to the court, and thus differ qualitatively from conditions informed by considerations other than the existence of legal authority, but which involve the legality or propriety of the exercise of the legal authority that was delegated. Thus, I largely subscribe to the position expressed by Professor Georges Abi-Saab, the dissenting arbitrator in *Abaclat* v. *Argentina*, who wrote that:

> [U]nder general international law, the two requirements in question [prior consultation and exhaustion or remedies] are considered as conditions of admissibility. But when such conditions are included in the Jurisdictional title, they condition, like any other reservation inserted in the jurisdictional title, the consent of the party or parties making them, to submit to the jurisdiction of the judicial or arbitral organ, and limit by that much the exercise by the organ of its jurisdiction. In other words, in this case these conditions become conventionally jurisdictional, in addition to being admissibility conditions by their legal nature.[16]

I am not convinced that conditions which limit the power of an International Centre for the Settlement of Investment Disputes (ICSID) tribunal to exercise jurisdiction, such as the need to engage in consultation to adjudication and to exhaust domestic remedies are 'by their legal nature' conditions of admissibility. However, I am in full agreement with Abi-Saab that the inclusion of such conditions in the jurisdictional title transforms them, in effect, into jurisdictional conditions – that is, conditions delineating the authority of the tribunal to adjudicate. If these conditions are not met, there is no legal authority to adjudicate, and if they are met, then in the absence

[16] *Abaclat* v. *Argentina*, ICSID Case No. ARB/07/5, dissenting opinion of Professor Abi-Saab of 28 October 2011, at para 23.

of other relevant considerations the tribunal must adjudicate the dispute.

In the same vein, I would maintain that several conditions referred to in the relevant constitutive instruments or in judicial practice as conditions of admissibility actually constitute jurisdictional conditions. These include the principle of complementarity as formulated in the International Criminal Court (ICC) Statute, which deprives the court of the power to adjudicate cases that have been genuinely investigated or litigated before a domestic court;[17] the 'six month rule' listed in the European Convention on Human Rights (ECHR), which excludes delayed applications from the jurisdiction of the European Court of Human Rights (ECtHR);[18] the 60 days rule found in the World Trade Organization (WTO) Dispute Settlement Understanding (DSU);[19] and the exhaustion of alternative dispute-settlement mechanism found in the compromissory clause of the Convention on the Elimination of Racial Discrimination (CERD), barring premature requests for the establishment of a dispute-settlement procedure.[20] All these are jurisdictional conditions governing the exercise of jurisdictional authority, in a manner circumscribing the delegation of adjudicative powers. Such conditions do not create exceptions to an existing jurisdictional title, but help to define and delineate the jurisdictional power conferred to the court to begin with. As a result, the fulfilment of these conditions must be established before the relevant international court in the same manner in which other aspects of its jurisdictional authority should be established.[21]

Admissibility considerations

While conditions appertaining to the jurisdictional clause are typically jurisdictional in nature, since they define and delineate

[17] ICC Statute, art. 17. [18] ECHR, art. 35. [19] DSU, art. 5.

[20] Convention on the Elimination of All Forms of Racial Discrimination, 21 December 1965, in force 4 January 1969, art. 22, 660 UNTS 195.

[21] See e.g., HRC, *Husseini* v. *Denmark*, Communication No. 2243/2013, U.N. Doc. CCPR/C/112/D/2243/2013 (2014), para 1, Joint opinion of Committee members Shany and Seetulsingh (dissenting) ('it is up to the Committee to ascertain that the author has exhausted all available domestic remedies, even if the State party has not explicitly raised the matter on its own'). Note that the majority on the Committee was of the view that the failure by the state to explicitly invoke the exhaustion claim constituted an implied waiver of the claim.

the scope of adjudicative power conferred upon international courts, there are certain limits on the exercise of jurisdiction of international courts, which do not negate the existence of adjudicative power. These are legal powers to decline to exercise jurisdiction, which may have been granted to international courts explicitly or implicitly, through the constitutive instruments or other sources of international law that govern the legality of the exercise of jurisdiction (but not necessarily the delegated authority to do so).

First, certain jurisdiction-conferring instruments explicitly provide international courts with discretion whether or not to hear certain cases, thus implying that the parties conferred upon the court both the power to adjudicate and the power to decide not to exercise the power to adjudicate under certain circumstances. For example, Protocol 14 to the ECHR authorizes the ECtHR to dismiss applications brought by individuals who have suffered an insignificant disadvantage 'unless respect for human rights as defined in the Convention and the Protocols thereto requires an examination of the application on the merits'.[22] In other words, the Court is entrusted with discretion to weigh whether respect for human rights merits the exercise of its power in *de minimis* cases which fall under its jurisdiction.

In the same vein, article 53 of the ICC Statute authorizes the ICC Prosecutor to terminate an investigation if doing so would serve the interests of justice, a decision that is partly reviewable before the Court.[23] Again, this provision does not modify the Court's jurisdiction, but rather allows the Court to decide not to exercise its power to adjudicate a case due to overriding considerations, not necessary of a legal nature (i.e. interests of justice).

Finally, article 65 of the ICJ Statute, which regulates the ICJ's advisory competence, provides that '[t]he Court *may* give an advisory opinion on any legal question at the request of whatever body may be authorized by or in accordance with the Charter of the United Nations to make such a request' (emphasis added). The use of the permissive term 'may', rather than the mandatory term 'shall', has led the Court to hold that it has discretion whether or not to refuse to issue an advisory opinion, but that given its role as the UN's principal judicial organ, it should decline jurisdiction for compelling reasons only.[24]

22 ECHR, art. 35(3)(b). 23 ICC Statute, art. 53(3).

24 See e.g., *Reservations to the Convention on the Prevention and Punishment of the Crime of Genocide*, 1951 ICJ 15, 19; *Legal Consequences for States of the Continued Presence of*

Admissibility conditions investing international courts with discretion not to exercise jurisdiction may also derive from sources other than the courts' own constitutive instruments. Among these sources, one can mention treaties in force between the parties (other than the constitutive instruments of international courts), general international law norms and, arguably, discretionary powers that may comprise part of the inherent powers possessed by international courts. Specifically, an international court, which has been granted with a jurisdictional title to adjudicate a certain dispute, may nonetheless rely on its inherent powers and decline to exercise this legal authority in situations where the exercise of adjudicative power would conflict with another applicable norm of international law.

Preserving legality

In *Minority Schools in Upper Silesia* the PCIJ held that:

> The Court's jurisdiction depends on the will of the parties. The Court is always competent once the latter have accepted its jurisdiction, since there is no dispute which States entitled to appear before the Court cannot refer to it ... This principle only becomes *inoperative in those exceptional cases* in which the dispute which States may desire to refer to the Court would fall within the exclusive jurisdiction reserved to some other authority.[25]

In other words, the Court took the view that it would be barred from exercising jurisdiction, notwithstanding the existence of legal authority, if this would result in a violation of a legal arrangement found in another legal instrument requiring the parties to refer the dispute to another dispute-settlement authority. Under these circumstances, the Court remains invested with jurisdiction, but the exercise of such jurisdiction becomes inoperative – that is, non-exercisable. Arguably, it is the very nature of international courts as rule of law institutions that supports the position that they have an inherent power to decline jurisdiction when adjudicating the case would result

South Africa in Namibia (South West Africa) notwithstanding Security Council Resolution 276, 1971 ICJ 16, 27.

25 *Rights of Minorities in Upper Silesia (Minority Schools)* (*Germany* v. *Poland*), 1928 PCIJ (ser A) No 15, at 22–23 (emphasis added).

in a violation of an international law norm (such as the violation of an exclusive jurisdiction clause).[26]

However, it is worth noting that some international courts have in the past been willing to issue substantive judgments explicitly running contrary to international norms found in sources independent of their constitutive treaties.[27] We cannot, therefore, rule out the possibility that they might also decide to exercise jurisdiction, at least under certain circumstances, in contravention of a norm of international law situated outside the purview of their specific legal regime.[28] Such an outcome can only be legally feasible were we to regard the external international law norm as appertaining not to the court's legal authority to adjudicate, but rather to the propriety of its doing so.

Further examples of an international court declining to exercise jurisdiction validly conferred upon it can be found in the ICJ's judgments in *Monetary Gold* and *East Timor.* In both cases, the Court held that it ought not to exercise its jurisdiction over disputes directly implicating the rights and interests of third parties, since doing so would cause the Court to adjudicate on these rights and interests in

[26] See e.g., Ernst-Ulrich Petersmann, 'Judicial Standards of Review and Administration of Justice in Trade and Investment Law and Adjudication', in Lukasz Gruszczynski and Wouter Werner (eds.), *Deference in International Courts and Tribunals: Standard of Review and Margin of Appreciation* (New York: Oxford University Press, 2014), p. 25. Note that the duty to ensure the application of international law derived from sources other than the constitutive instrument of the relevant international court can sometimes be derived, explicitly or implicitly, from the constitutive instruments themselves. For example, see Treaty on the European Union, Maastricht, 7 February 1992, in force 1 November 1993, art. 19, OJ (C326) 13 (Consolidated Version of 26 October 2012) ('[The Court of Justice] shall ensure that in the interpretation and application of the Treaties the law is observed'); ICC Statute, art. 98; Treaty of the South African Development Community, 17 August 1992, 30 September 1993, art. 4(c), www.sadc.int/files/9113/5292/9434/SADC_Treaty.pdf.

[27] See e.g., Joined cases C-402/05 P and C-415/05 P, *Kadi* v. *Council* [2008] ECR-I 6351, at para 285 ('the obligations imposed by an international agreement cannot have the effect of prejudicing the constitutional principles of the EC Treaty'); *Argentina – Definitive Anti-Dumping Duties on Poultry from Brazil,* Report of the Panel of 22 April 2003, WTO Doc. WT/DS241/R (2003), at para 7.41 ('we see no reason at all why we should be bound by the rulings of non-WTO dispute settlement bodies').

[28] The question of whether the WTO Dispute Settlement Mechanism could exercise jurisdiction in circumstances where the parties have undertaken to litigate elsewhere has been left open by the Appellate Body. *Mexico – Tax Measures on Soft Drinks and Other Beverages,* Report of the AB of 6 March 2006, WTO Doc. WT/DS308/AB/R, at para 54.

the absence of consent to adjudication by the relevant third parties.[29] The need to respect the principle of consent led the Court to decline jurisdiction so as not to facilitate a violation of a basic principle of general international law.

Here too, however, some international courts have demonstrated less timidity in adjudicating cases directly implicating the rights and interests of third parties without their consent to adjudication, underscoring the discretionary nature of this ground of admissibility.[30] Furthermore, even the ICJ itself did not follow the same line of reasoning in requests for advisory opinions and exercised its advisory jurisdiction notwithstanding the opposition of the states whose rights and interests were directly implicated in these decisions.[31] Arguably, the non-binding nature of advisory opinions – which do not involve adjudication *stricto senso* – served to mitigate the conflict between the exercise of jurisdiction and the principle of consent to adjudication.

Protecting the judicial function

A further justification for declining jurisdiction found in judicial practice is the need to protect the judicial function. Arguably, international courts are invested with certain inherent powers that derive from their judicial attributes even if their constitutive instruments do not allude to these powers.[32] These inherent powers may include the power to decline jurisdiction in order to protect the judicial function and to ensure the sound administration of justice. One can find strong support for this legal construction in two ICJ cases dealing with moot applications, with regard to which the Court took the view that issuing judgments which will have no legal effect or which are legally unnecessary would be incompatible

[29] *Monetary Gold Removed from Rome in 1943* (*Italy* v. *France*), 1954 ICJ 19, 32 ('To adjudicate upon the international responsibility of Albania without her consent would run counter to a well-established principle of international law embodied in the Court's Statute, namely, that the Court can only exercise jurisdiction over a State with its consent'); *East Timor* (*Portugal* v. *Australia*), 1995 ICJ 90, 104–105.

[30] See e.g., *Soering* v. *UK*, 161 Eur. Ct. H.R. (ser. A) (1989) (review of US criminal law and procedure and prison conditions without its consent).

[31] See e.g., Western Sahara, 1975 ICJ 12, 24–25; Legal Consequences of the Construction of a Wall in the Occupied Palestinian Territory, 2004 ICJ 136, 157–158.

[32] See Chester Brown, *A Common Law of International Adjudication* (New York: Oxford University Press, 2007), p. 70; Gleider Hernendez, *The International Court of Justice and the Judicial Function* (New York: Oxford University Press, 2014), p. 51.

with its judicial function.[33] In fact, in *Northern Cameroons*, the Court explicitly stated the proposition that its inherent power to protect its jurisdiction may justify its decline of a validly conferred jurisdictional title:

> [E]ven if the Court, when seised, finds that it has jurisdiction, the Court is not compelled in every case to exercise that jurisdiction. There are inherent limitations on the exercise of the judicial function which the Court, as a court of justice, can never ignore. There may thus be an incompatibility between the desires of an applicant, or, indeed, of both parties to a case, on the one hand, and on the other hand the duty of the Court to maintain its judicial character. The Court itself, and not the parties, must be the guardian of the Court's judicial integrity.[34]

In the same vein, it held in *Nuclear Tests* that:

> Such inherent jurisdiction, on the basis of which the Court is fully empowered to make whatever findings may be necessary for the purposes just indicated, derives from the mere existence of the Court as a judicial organ established by the consent of States, and is conferred upon it in order that its basic judicial functions may be safeguarded.[35]

Another application of the theory of inherent power to decline jurisdiction can be observed in cases dealing with abusive applications which appear to be brought in bad faith or are manifestly ill-founded. For instance, an ICSID Tribunal refused to hear a case validly referred to it due to the bad faith demonstrated by the investor. Although the ICSID Convention and the relevant bilateral investment treaty (BIT) were silent on the matter, the Tribunal held that the state parties to ICSID could not have intended to subject

[33] *Northern Cameroons* (*Cameroon* v. *UK*), 1963 ICJ 15, 33–34:

> The function of the Court is to state the law, but it may pronounce judgment only in connection with concrete cases where there exists at the time of the adjudication an actual controversy involving a conflict of legal interests between the parties. The Court's judgment must have some practical consequence in the sense that it can affect existing legal rights or obligations of the parties, thus removing uncertainty from their legal relations. No judgment on the merits in this case could satisfy these essentials of the judicial function.

Nuclear Tests (*Australia* v. *France*), 1974 ICJ 253, 271: 'The Court therefore sees no reason to allow the continuance of proceedings which it knows are bound to be fruitless. While judicial settlement may provide a path to international harmony in circumstances of conflict, it is none the less true that the needless continuance of litigation is an obstacle to such harmony'.

[34] *Northern Cameroons* (*Cameroon* v. *UK*), 1963 ICJ 15, 29.

[35] *Nuclear Tests* (*Australia* v. *France*), 1974 ICJ 253, 259–260.

themselves to abusive adjudication and that, accordingly, it was without jurisdiction.[36] A further example can be found in the ICJ's decision in the request for provisional measures in *Use of Force (NATO)*, in which the Court invoked without a textual basis in the constitutive instruments the manifestly ill-founded nature of the application – that is, the far-fetched character of the accusation that NATO forces were committing genocide in Yugoslavia – as a reason to find the absence of *prima facie* jurisdiction and not to issue provisional measures in the case.[37]

Sequencing of preliminary objections

If objections to admissibility are indeed qualitatively different to objections to jurisdiction – the former relating to the exercise of legal authority and the latter to the existence of legal authority – then one would expect that objections to admissibility will be raised only after it has already been established that a Court is *authorized* to hear the case, and before the adjudication of the merits of the case. In practice, however, international courts have not always kept this sequence. In *Northern Cameroons*, for instance, the application was found to be inadmissible without the ICJ pronouncing on the respondent's jurisdictional objections.[38] As in the case of judicial

[36] *Phoenix Action Ltd* v. *Czech Republic*, ICSID Case No. ARB/06/5, Award of 15 April 2009, at para 106 ('In the Tribunal's view, States cannot be deemed to offer access to the ICSID dispute settlement mechanism to investments not made in good faith. The protection of international investment arbitration cannot be granted if such protection would run contrary to the general principles of international law, among which the principle of good faith is of utmost importance'). Admittedly, the Tribunal's reasoning does not perfectly fit the structure proposed in this chapter, as it invoked both lack of authorization (the parties could not have intended to authorize the Tribunal to hear abusive cases) and the violation of a basic principle of international law (i.e., the principle of good faith). Still, I regard the prevention of abuse of process as closely tied to the need to protect the integrity of the judicial process and the judicial function.

[37] *Legality of Use of Force* (*Serbia and Montenegro* v. *Belgium*), 1999 ICJ 124, 138 (provisional measures):

> Whereas the Court is therefore not in a position to find, at this stage of the proceedings, that the acts imputed by Yugoslavia to the Respondent are capable of coming within the provisions of the Genocide Convention; and whereas Article IX of the Convention, invoked by Yugoslavia, cannot accordingly constitute a basis on which the jurisdiction of the Court could prima facie be founded in this case.

[38] *Northern Cameroons* (*Cameroon* v. *UK*), 1963 ICJ 15, 27 ('the Court does not find it necessary to consider all the objections, nor to determine whether all of them are objections to jurisdiction or to admissibility or based on other grounds').

decisions to qualify a jurisdictional question raising issues intertwined with the merits of the case as being not of a preliminary nature,[39] and as with decisions to hear certain substantive issues having a preliminary character before delving into the merits of the case,[40] it appears that international courts also enjoy some discretion in sequencing admissibility issues. They may thus decide to hear them before objecting to jurisdiction, or join them to the merits of the case.

Such an exercise of discretion relating to sequencing of the parties' claims is possible because international courts have been willing to assume in proceedings involving objections to admissibility, as in cases involving ancillary powers, that *prima facie* jurisdiction exists.[41] Thus, the ICJ or other international courts have not generally followed the position expressed by Judge Lauterpacht in his dissenting opinion in *Interhandel*, namely that jurisdictional issues must be resolved before questions of admissibility are to be addressed.[42] This is a sensible approach, since following a strict order of sequencing of preliminary objections would unnecessarily complicate the proceedings by requiring international courts to designate a separate procedural stage for each objection,[43] and by limiting the power of the Court to quickly dispose of ill-founded cases. The upshot of this is that classifying a preliminary objection

[39] See ICJ Rules, rule 79(9); European Court of Human Rights, Rules of Court, 1 July 2014, Rule 54A.

[40] See *South West Africa* (*Ethiopia* v. *South Africa*), 1966 ICJ 6, 18. For criticism, see *ibid.*, at 240 (dissenting opinion of Judge Koretzky) ('The Court . . . has thereby reverted from the stage of the merits to the stage of jurisdiction'); *ibid.*, at 382 (dissenting opinion by Judge Jessup):

> Why would the Court tolerate a situation in which the parties would be put to great trouble and expense to explore all the details of the merits, and only thereafter be told that the Court would pay no heed to all their arguments and evidence because the case was dismissed on a preliminary ground which precluded any investigation of the merits?

[41] See Thirlway, 'The Law and Procedure of International Courts and Tribunals', 140–141.

[42] *Interhandel* (*Switzerland* v. *US*), 1959 ICJ 6, 100 (Lauterpacht J., dissenting) ('according to the established practice of the Court preliminary objections must be examined–and rejected–before the plea of admissibility is examined').

[43] See e.g., Fitzmaurice, 'Jurisdiction, Competence and Procedure', 57–58, 108 (designating proceedings on whether there is a dispute as a preliminary question of jurisdiction – distinct from 'substantive' jurisdictional issues, and referring to interim measures as 'pre-preliminary' in nature).

as relating to a question of admissibility does not necessarily determine its sequencing order.

Burden of proof

Another, more significant, implication of the distinction between jurisdiction and admissibility objections pertains to the burden of proof imposed on the parties. Generally speaking, international courts operate in accordance with the maxim of *onus probandi incumbit actori*, placing the burden of proof of an argument on the party that raises the argument.[44] With respect to jurisdictional matters, the traditional approach of the World Court has been that the burden to establish the Court's jurisdiction typically lies with the applicant party. This outcome is no doubt a reflection of the exceptional nature of international adjudication before the Court, as was indeed explained by the PCIJ in *Chorzow Factory* in the context of the weight of evidence sought by the Court:

> It is true that the Court's jurisdiction is always a limited one, existing only in so far as States have accepted it; consequently, the Court will, in the event of an objection–or when it has automatically to consider the question–only affirm its jurisdiction provided that the force of the arguments militating in favour of it is preponderant.[45]

Fitzmaurice even went beyond this formulation and argued that consent to jurisdiction – that is, specific jurisdiction – must be established 'beyond reasonable doubt'.[46] This proposed standard appears to me to be difficult to justify since it seems to lead to a peculiar result, whereby the procedural norm containing the acceptance of an international court's adjudicative power would, at times, be subject to a higher evidentiary threshold than the substantive rights and obligations whose interpretation and application have been put to adjudication. Still, the preponderance of evidence standard implies that with respect to questions of foundational

[44] *Pulp Mills on the River Uruguay* (*Argentina* v. *Uruguay*), 2010 ICJ 14, 71; *Asian Agricultural Products Ltd. (Aapl)* v. *Sri Lanka*, Case No. ARB/87/3 (1991) *6 ICSID Review – Foreign Investment Law Journal* 526, 549; *US – Measure Affecting Imports of Woven Wool Shirts and Blouses from India*, Appellate Body Report of 15 April 1997, WTO Doc. WT/DS33/AB/R (1997), at 16–17.

[45] *Factory at Chorzów* (*Germany* v. *Poland*), 1927 PCIJ (ser A) No 9, at 32.

[46] Fitzmaurice, 'Jurisdiction, Competence and Procedure', 11.

jurisdiction, such as access to the court (foundational jurisdiction *ratione personae*), which the parties cannot waive or stipulate upon, the burden may rest on the applicant even when the respondent party fails to raise an objection to jurisdiction. The reason for this is that international courts may need to establish their foundational jurisdiction *proprio motu*, and would be required to dismiss the case unless the preponderance of evidence points in the direction of their having jurisdiction.[47]

However, at the admissibility stage, when a claim is raised that an international court should refrain from exercising the power, which was conferred upon it by the parties, I believe that the *onus probandi incumbit actori* rule supports shifting the burden of proof to the shoulders of the respondent. Such an outcome is consistent with the view that admissibility constitutes an exception to jurisdiction – that is, that in the absence of a special justification, international courts should exercise jurisdiction – and with the tendency to allocate the burden of proof to the party arguing for an exception to a rule.[48] It is interesting to note that in a 2002 Report by the ILC Special Rapporteur on Diplomatic Protection, Professor John Dugard proposed to impose the burden of proof that local remedies were not exhausted in diplomatic protection cases on the respondent party, and the burden of proving exception to the exhaustion rule upon the applicant.[49] This arrangement was omitted from the final version of the Draft Articles after some members of the ILC expressed doubt as to whether it reflects customary international law.[50] The confusion as to who should bear the burden of establishing the rule of exhaustion may reflect the difficulties in classifying this rule and from the conflicting guidance derived from the principles that jurisdictional conditions should, as a rule, be established

[47] See e.g., *Appeal Relating to the Jurisdiction of the ICAO Council* (*India* v. *Pakistan*), 1972 ICJ 46, 52 ('The Court must however always be satisfied that it has jurisdiction, and must if necessary go into that matter *proprio motu*'); *Legality of Use of Force*, 2004 ICJ at 299 (suggesting that the Court must first of all examine questions of access to the Court).

[48] See *US-Wool Shirts*, note 44, 16 (party arguing an exception in the form of an affirmative defence needs to carry the burden of proving it).

[49] Third report on diplomatic protection, by Mr John Dugard, Special Rapporteur, 7 March–16 April 2002, at 72–75, UN Doc. A/CN.4/523 and Add.1 (2002).

[50] Report of the International Law Commission, 54th Sess. (29 April–7 June and 22 July–16 August 2002), para 246, UN Doc. A/57/10 (2002).

by the applicant and that positive claims challenging the exercise of jurisdiction should be substantiated by the party raising them (typically, the respondent party).

In summary, designating a claim as a challenge to the admissibility of a case, as opposed to jurisdiction over it, may imply a change in the order in which it would be processed and in the allocation of burdens of proof. It does not imply, however, that it is more or less prone to waiver or more or less 'curable' in the event of a failure to meet the necessary conditions. Whereas some jurisdictional requirements may be waived or cured (e.g. exhaustion of local remedies or initial lack of party consent to adjudicate a specific question), others cannot be waived or cured (e.g. the right of access to the court or gravity requirements);[51] and, similarly, some admissibility claims are waivable (such as an agreement to adjudicate before another international tribunal),[52] while others are not (e.g. mootness or claims directly implicating the rights and interests of third parties).

The most significant distinction between jurisdiction and admissibility, however, would appear to be conceptual in nature. The scope of jurisdictional authority and the jurisdictional conditions appertaining thereto have been predetermined by the mandate providers and the parties to the case. The task of the relevant international court is to interpret and apply these requirements, engaging thereby in category-based case selection (e.g. determining what would constitute an 'investment' or a crime of sufficient gravity), which would apply to all cases – past, present and future.

As the next and final chapter suggests, admissibility criteria relating to the propriety of exercising adjudicative authority tend to be more discretionary in nature and more attuned to the particular circumstances of the dispute at hand, thus facilitating more specific case selection, determined by the relevant international court (and not predetermined by the mandate providers or the disputing parties). Over time, however, the differences between holdings on

[51] ICC Statute, art. 17(1)(d). See Jann K Kleffner, 'Auto Referrals and the Complementary Nature of the ICC', in Stahn and Sluiter (eds.), *The Emerging Practice of the International Criminal Court*, p. 46.

[52] See e.g., North American Free Trade Agreement, 17 December 1992, in force 1 January 1994, art. 2005, 32 ILM (1993) 289 and 605 (authorizing respondent parties to insist on adjudication before NAFTA, in certain circumstances).

jurisdiction and holdings on admissibility may be eroded, as discretionary rulings will also tend to follow a predictable course.[53] This will result in effect in category-based case selection in admissibility cases, albeit typically on the basis of standards introduced by the international court itself.

[53] *Cf.* Richard A Posner, *How Judges Think* (Cambridge, MA: Harvard University Press, 2010), p. 87.

11

Admissibility as a policy tool

Judicial propriety

To view admissibility as a power held by an international court, enabling it, under certain circumstances, to decline to exercise its powers of adjudication invites questions as to the motivations that may explain the manner in which this power not to exercise power is employed. An understanding of the policies which drive the application of admissibility requirements may, perhaps, help us to anticipate how international courts are likely to select cases in future. Such an understanding may also provide us with opportunities for a critical evaluation of such policies and of the way in which they are advanced by the employment of admissibility criteria.

One set of policies advanced by admissibility standards pertains to judicial propriety – that is, the need to conduct judicial business in ways conducive to the preservation of judicial legitimacy. This is sometimes referred to in the International Court of Justice (ICJ) case law as protection of the judicial function or integrity.[1] It could be argued that international courts derive important components of their legitimacy from the separation between politics and law and their association with the latter, rather than the former;[2] from the

[1] *Northern Cameroons* (*Cameroon* v. *UK*), 1963 ICJ 15, 29 ('There may thus be an incompatibility between the desires of an applicant, or, indeed, of both parties to a case, on the one hand, and on the other hand the duty of the Court to maintain its judicial character. The Court itself, and not the parties, must be the guardian of the Court's judicial integrity').

[2] See e.g. J G Merrills, *International Dispute Settlement*, 5th edn. (Cambridge: Cambridge University Press, 2011), p. 155; Michelle L Burgis, *Boundaries of Discourse in the International Court of Justice: Mapping Arguments in Arab Territorial*

continued hold of certain myths about the operation of the judiciary such as judicial independence and impartiality;[3] and from their status as guardians of the rule of law.[4] It may also be claimed that the process of adjudication is a legitimate method for settling disputes and resolving international problems since it is consistent with fundamental notions of procedural fairness and substantive justice.[5] Once an international court is faced with a case that threatens this set of images and perceptions, it should arguably have the power to defend itself from being dragged down a harmful procedural road. Such protective powers are either recognized in the relevant court's constitutive instruments, or, more typically, recognized as part of its inherent or implicit powers.

One rather straightforward example of an admissibility provision designed to protect judicial propriety is article 35(3)(a) of the European Convention on Human Rights (ECtHR), which allows the Court to reject applications as inadmissible if they constitute an abuse of the right of individual application.[6] The prohibition of abuse in this context enables the ECtHR to extricate itself from proceedings which may be unfair or lead to unjust results.[7]

Disputes (Leiden: Martinus Nijhoff Publishers, 2009), pp. 42–43; Alexander Orakhelashvili, *The Interpretation of Acts and Rules in Public International Law* (New York: Oxford University Press, 2008), p. 35.

3 See e.g. Marcel Storme, 'Independence of the Judiciary: The European Perspective', in Shimon Shetreet and Christopher Forsyth (eds.), *The Culture of Judicial Independence* (Leiden: Martinus Nijhoff Publishers, 2012), pp. 90–91; John Bell, *Judiciaries with Europe: A Comparative Review* (Cambridge: Cambridge University Press, 2006), p. 342.

4 See e.g. Jan Klabbers, *International Law* (Cambridge: Cambridge University Press, 2013), p. 311; Gleider Hernendez, *The International Court of Justice and the Judicial Function* (New York: Oxford University Press, 2014), p. 196.

5 See e.g. Thomas M Franck, 'Fairness in International Legal and Institutional System: General Course on Public International Law' (1994) 240 *Recueil Des Cours, Collected Courses 1993-III* 12, 302–303; Luiz Eduardo Salles, *Forum Shopping in International Adjudication: The Role of Preliminary Objections* (Cambridge: Cambridge University Press, 2014), p. 61; VS Mani, *International Adjudication Procedural Aspects* (The Hague: Martinus Nijhoff Publishers, 1980), p. 2.

6 ECHR, art. 35(3) reads: 'The Court shall declare inadmissible any individual application submitted under Article 34 if it considers that: (a) the application is incompatible with the provisions of the Convention or the Protocols thereto, manifestly ill-founded, or an abuse of the right of individual application'. See also UNCLOS, art. 294.

7 See e.g. Andrew L-T Choo, *The Abuse of Process Doctrine and Criminal Justice*, 2nd edn. (New York: Oxford University Press, 2008), p. 18.

The mootness of an adjudicated claim may offer another example of the application of judicial power which may harm the legitimacy of an international court, since it inevitably leads to judgments which do not change reality, thereby portraying adjudication as hypothetical or inconsequential in nature. In *Foglia* v. *Novello*, for example, the Court of Justice of the European Union (CJEU) held that it would be improper to utilize the process of preliminary rulings for challenging the lawfulness of practices taken by another member state, writing that:

> The duty assigned to the court by article 177 is not that of delivering advisory opinions on general or hypothetical questions but of assisting in the administration of justice in the member states. It accordingly does not have jurisdiction to reply to questions of interpretation which are submitted to it within the framework of procedural devices arranged by the parties in order to induce the court to give its views on certain problems of community law which do not correspond to an objective requirement inherent in the resolution of a dispute. A declaration by the court that it has no jurisdiction in such circumstances does not in any way trespass upon the prerogatives of the national court but makes it possible to prevent the application of the procedure under article 177 for purposes other than those appropriate for it.[8]

Although the CJEU held that it lacks *jurisdiction* in the circumstances of the case to entertain the request for a preliminary ruling, the allusion in the judgment to the inappropriateness of applications which were brought within the correct legal framework, but would not serve the procedure's purpose, suggests that it was actually considering an issue of *admissibility*. According to the judgment, utilization of preliminary ruling procedures for purposes other than those intrinsic to adjudicating a concrete dispute involving the member state whose organs submitted the request should lead the Court to employ what must be an inherent power to decline to exercise its jurisdiction in order to protect its proper judicial function.

The World Court has also taken the approach that it has inherent powers to determine the inadmissibility of applications which stand in tension with notions of judicial propriety. In the 1929 *Free Zones* case, the Permanent Court of International Justice (PCIJ) opined in *obiter dicta* that its duty to preserve its judicial function may require it to ignore an agreement by the adjudicating parties, which would seek to limit the power of the Court to pronounce the law, would subject

[8] Case C-244/80, *Foglia* v. *Novello* [1981] ECR 3045, 3062–3063.

its judgment to the parties' approval, or require it to adjudicate a legal case on the basis of non-legal interests.[9]

In the same vein, the ICJ held in *Northern Cameroons* that it should decline jurisdiction when confronted with what is essentially a moot case – an application asking the Court to pronounce on past illegalities, without seeking a remedy other than a declaration of illegality:

> The function of the Court is to state the law, but it may pronounce judgment only in connection with concrete cases where there exists at the time of the adjudication an actual controversy involving a conflict of legal interests between the parties. The Court's judgment must have some practical consequence in the sense that it can affect existing legal rights or obligations of the parties, thus removing uncertainty from their legal relations. No judgment on the merits in this case could satisfy these essentials of the judicial function.[10]

It should be noted that, unlike some of the cases discussed earlier, there was no real suggestion that Cameroon's application constituted an abuse of the legal process before the Court. Nor is it clear that its application interfered with fundamental notions of fairness or justice (such as the need to protect the rights and interests of third parties). Instead, it appears that the invocation of the Court's inherent power to protect its judicial function derived from the Court's need to preserve its image as a judicial institution of consequence, invested with a dominant dispute-settling function, and which serves the maintenance of international peace and security.[11] Another possible consideration may be that of judicial economy, militating against the employment of scarce judicial resources for what may be, from a practical point of view, a pointless judicial exercise.[12]

These considerations are not completely convincing, however. Both before and after the *Northern Cameroons* case, the Court has issued declaratory judgments in the course of settling contentious

[9] *The Free Zones of Upper Savoy and the District Of Get* (*France* v. *Switzerland*), 1932 PCIJ (ser A/B) No 46, at 138, 161–162.

[10] *Northern Cameroons* (*Cameroon* v. *UK*), 1963 ICJ 15, 33–34.

[11] See e.g. Nagendra Singh, *The Role and Record of the International Court of Justice* (Dordrecht: Martinus Nijhoff Publishers, 1989), p. 130; Serena Forlati, *The International Court of Justice: An Arbitral Tribunal or a Judicial Body* (Cham: Springer International Publishing, 2014), p. 122.

[12] See e.g. Hugh Thirlway, 'Judicial Activism and the International Court of Justice', in Nisuke Ando *et al.* (eds.), *Judge Shigeru Oda: Liber Amicorum* (The Hague: Kluwer Law International, 2002), pp. 77–78.

cases, and it is not clear whether one can regard some of the declarations in cases such as *Corfu Channel*[13] or *Application of the Genocide Convention (Bosnia* v. *Serbia)*[14] as more forward looking than the declaration sought in *Northern Cameroons*.[15] It is also questionable what makes an application for a declarative judgment incompatible with the international judicial function in a system of law where declarative forms of satisfaction infused with little practical dimension, including apologies and expressions of regret, constitute possible remedies.[16] Furthermore, the position that a theoretic articulation of international law is incompatible with the international judicial function is particularly hard to sustain for a court such as the ICJ, which is explicitly invested with advisory jurisdiction. In fact, some of the criticism directed at the ICJ in recent decades has argued that even in advisory proceedings, such as the *Nuclear Weapons*[17] and *Kosovo* cases,[18] its pronouncements of abstract legal principles were too narrow, bordering on the pointless.[19]

In summary, I find myself in agreement with Judge Badawi, one of the dissenting judges in *Northern Cameroons*, who expressed bewilderment at the Court's decision to decline to issue a declarative judgment without a practical remedy in this case, while not acting in this manner in other cases. I also find it difficult to believe that in 1963,

[13] *Corfu Channel* (*UK* v. *Albania*), 1949 ICJ 4, 35.

[14] *Application of the Convention on the Prevention and Punishment of the Crime of Genocide* (*Bosnia and Herzegovina* v. *Serbia and Montenegro*), 2007 ICJ 43, 235–236.

[15] See *Northern Cameroons* (*Cameroon* v. *UK*), 1963 ICJ 15, 150–151 (dissenting opinion of Judge Badawi):

> The Court does not cite the Corfu Channel case ... [This] case is almost identical with the present one. But to declare that the present case is inadmissible as a result of the termination of the trusteeship, because it could not lead to any practical application, is to assume that the essential feature of any legal action is that it must have a practical application. This assumption is undeniable where a judgment is sought for the purposes of execution, but it is more than questionable in the case of declaratory judgments.

[16] Draft articles on Responsibility of States for Internationally Wrongful Acts, art. 37(2), Annex to General Assembly Resolution 56/83 of 12 December 2001, GAOR 56th Sess., Sup No 10 (A/56/10), Chapter 5.

[17] *Legality of the Threat or Use of Nuclear Weapons*, 1995 ICJ 226, 263.

[18] *Accordance with International Law of the Unilateral Declaration of Independence in respect of Kosovo*, 2010 ICJ 403, 438.

[19] See e.g. Kati Kulovesi, 'Legality or Otherwise? Nuclear Weapons and the Strategy of *Non Liquet*' (2002) 10 *Finnish Yearbook of International Law* 55, 70–72; Theodore Christakis, 'The ICJ Advisory Opinion on Kosovo: Has International Law Something to Say about Secession?' (2011) 24 *Leiden Journal of International Law* 73, 75–76.

when the Court's docket of cases was almost empty, it was concerned about the need to prioritize other contentious cases for reasons of judicial economy. One can therefore speculate that other policy considerations were involved in the case and motivated the Court to construe its inherent powers to decline to adjudicate improper cases in a broad manner. Perhaps, the Court wished to avoid the highly charged controversies associated with the decolonization process (a similar concern may have led it to decline jurisdiction in *South West Africa* three years later); and perhaps the Court took the view that reviewing the legality of the international borders of Cameroon would not settle existing disputes, but rather create new ones.[20]

In any case, the lack of transparency with regard to the policy considerations applied by international courts may be one of the main disadvantages of expanding its ability to selectively vet specific cases on a discretionary basis. Yet, a decision by an international court *not* to exercise its discretionary powers may raise equally difficult problems of transparency – especially in cases where its decision on the substance smacks of an attempt to shirk its adjudicative function. The practice of the ICJ, which never declined to exercise advisory jurisdiction by reason of impropriety, on the one hand,[21] and has issued at times extremely narrow substantive opinions, on the other, could arguably be explained as involving certain hidden case selection considerations.

A subset of considerations of judicial propriety which may push international courts to employ their explicit, implicit or inherent powers to decline jurisdiction involves considerations of legality – that is, situations where the exercise of jurisdiction by a court may contradict an important principle of international law or legal norm. As mentioned before, the ICJ has in the past declined to exercise jurisdiction where it regarded such an exercise to run contrary to a central principle of international law (such as consent to adjudication),[22] while the PCIJ has opined that it should not

[20] See Singh, *The Role and Record of the International Court of Justice*, p. 130.

[21] The only request for advisory opinion, which was declined – the WHO's request in the *Use by a State of Nuclear Weapons* case – was rejected for lack of jurisdiction. *Legality of the Use by a State of Nuclear Weapons in Armed Conflict*, 1996 ICJ 66. The PCIJ did decline jurisdiction for lack of propriety in *Eastern Carelia*. *Status of Eastern Carelia*, 1923 PCIJ (Ser B) No 5.

[22] *Monetary Gold Removed from Rome in 1943* (*Italy* v. *France et al.*), 1954 ICJ 19.

exercise jurisdiction if this will violate an exclusive agreement investing jurisdiction over the same dispute with another dispute-settling institution.[23]

In protecting general international law principles and other international law institutions, international courts appear to be trying to protect their own legitimacy. Since international courts derive much of their authority from notions of the rule of law and from their perceived role as guardians of the international rule of law,[24] allowing parties to adjudication to utilize them in ways that violate substantive or procedural international law could undermine their own legitimacy. Declining jurisdictions under such circumstances may also encourage other courts to reciprocate and recognize the substantive or procedural rules of the legal regime in which the first-to-decline international court operates, further strengthening its authority vis-à-vis potential parties to adjudication.[25]

The policy choice taken by specialized international courts when confronted with considerations of legality may differ, however, from those of general international courts such as the ICJ. This is because specialized courts may prioritize the needs of their own legal regime over those of other legal regimes or general international law out of a sense of primary fidelity to the normative goals of the legal regime they serve.

In *Soering* v. *United Kingdom*, for example, a case dealing with the extradition of a suspected murderer to the United States, the ECtHR refused to apply a *Monetary Gold* type non-admissibility claim designed to protect the legal rights and interests of a third party who did not consent to the Court's jurisdiction. Since the applicant in the case claimed that his extradition to the United States would expose him to human rights violations and invited the Court to review the conditions of death row convicts in the United States, the United Kingdom argued that a ruling on the issue would entail adjudication over the responsibility of a non-member state. The Court, however, flatly rejected this argument:

[23] *Minority Schools*, 1928 PCIJ (Ser A) No 15, at 22–23. [24] See note 4.

[25] See e.g. Mohamed Bennouna, 'How to Cope with the Proliferation of International Courts and Coordinate Their Action', in Antonio Cassese (ed.), *Realizing Utopia: The Future of International Law* (Oxford: Oxford University Press, 2012), p. 292; Yuval Shany, *The Competing Jurisdictions of International Court* (New York: Oxford University Press, 2003), p. 261.

> [T]here is no question of adjudicating on or establishing the responsibility of the receiving country, whether under general international law, under the Convention or otherwise. In so far as any liability under the Convention is or may be incurred, it is liability incurred by the extraditing Contracting State by reason of its having taken action which has as a direct consequence the exposure of an individual to proscribed ill-treatment.[26]

This highly formalistic reasoning is not completely persuasive, since the Court could only assign responsibility to the United Kingdom after evaluating the compatibility with the European Court of Human Rights (ECHR) of the way in which the United States treats death row inmates. Such an examination directly implicates the legal interests of a state that has not accepted the jurisdiction of the ECtHR (nor has it accepted the standards provided for in the ECHR). Here too, it would seem that the Court prioritized policy considerations related to judicial legitimacy, and the ECtHR may have taken the view that the harm to the general international law principle of consent as the basis for adjudication would be outweighed by the need to ensure effective protection for the rights of individuals against treatment related to the distasteful death penalty. Indeed, the outsider status of the United States (its non-membership in the Council of Europe) may have actually limited the weight assigned to the *Monetary Gold* principle, since the Court did not feel obliged to protect its legal interests, being a non-Council of Europe state. In fact, infringing on the international law right of the United States, not to be adjudicated without its consent, may be regarded as a form of cost-externalization by the Court.

Admissibility as an effectiveness tool

Admissibility objections may also serve to enhance an international court's ability to attain its broader goals – that is, to increase its effectiveness.[27] Hence, the application of rules on admissibility may also be influenced by policy choices relating to the Court's substantive mandate and institutional welfare. One example of the utilization of an admissibility rule as an effectiveness tool is the ECtHR's practice of declining jurisdiction over manifestly ill-founded applications. By summarily dismissing 'weak' cases which do not appear to raise a serious

[26] *Soering* v. *UK*, 161 Eur. Ct. H.R. (ser. A) (1989), para 88.

[27] See Yuval Shany, *Assessing the Effectiveness of International Courts* (New York: Oxford University Press, 2014), pp. 13–14.

problem of implementation of the ECHR, the Court is able to prioritize the consideration of 'stronger' cases in which its involvement may meaningfully contribute towards improved protection of human rights in Europe.[28] Indeed, Stephen Greer noted that, even before the entry into force of Protocol 14, some 97 per cent of cases submitted to the Court were rejected as inadmissible – the ill-founded nature of the application being the most popular reason for dismissal.[29]

Still, Protocol 14 has further expanded the discretionary powers of the Court, allowing it to decline jurisdiction summarily even over well-founded applications in those cases where:

> [T]he applicant has not suffered a significant disadvantage, unless respect for human rights as defined in the Convention and the Protocols thereto requires an examination of the application on the merits and provided that no case may be rejected on this ground which has not been duly considered by a domestic tribunal.[30]

Unlike the criteria of gravity mentioned in article 17 of the Rome Statute, which I regard as a jurisdictional condition, since it delineates the Court's authority, excluding from its jurisdiction crimes that do not reach the gravity threshold and leaving the Court no discretion whether to adjudicate after the threshold had been set and met, the new power to decline jurisdiction under Protocol 14 to the ECHR goes to the case's admissibility. Under article 35(3)(b) to the Convention, even if the set conditions are met (the case involving an insignificant disadvantage to the applicant and due consideration by a domestic tribunal), the Court still has discretion to decide whether, in the particular circumstances, respect for human rights requires an examination of the case. In other words, the Court may decide whether or not to decline jurisdiction in the light of effectiveness considerations – the anticipated contribution of adjudication to promoting the normative goals of the Court.

Indeed, in one case involving a delay causing an insignificant disadvantage to the applicant (the lack of enforcement of a civil fine imposed against a city official), the Court decided to decline jurisdiction citing the following policy reasons:

[28] European Court of Human Rights, The Court's Priority Policy (2009), www.echr.coe.int/Documents/Priority_policy_ENG.pdf.

[29] Stephen Greer, *The European Convention on Human Rights: Achievements, Problems and Prospects* (Cambridge: Cambridge University Press, 2006), p. 174.

[30] ECHR, art. 35(3)(b).

The Court further observes that the problem of non-enforcement in Romania has been addressed on numerous occasions in its judgments ... The examination of this application on the merits would not introduce any new element in this regard ... The Court therefore concludes that respect for human rights as defined in the Convention and its Protocols does not require an examination of the application on the merits.[31]

In other words, effectiveness considerations – the improbability that a judgment on the merits of the case would advance the Court's mission of promoting the implementation of the relevant Convention right in Romania – led it to regard the case as inadmissible. One may easily imagine another set of circumstances (e.g. an identical case involving a different state), where the normative aims of the Court would militate in favour of exercising jurisdiction.

A similar set of considerations may underlie some of the decisions by the ICJ to decline jurisdiction. For instance, it may well be the case that both in the aforementioned *Northern Cameroons*, where the applicant did not seek an operative remedy,[32] and in *Nuclear Tests*, where the Court held that the French president's undertaking not to conduct further atmospheric nuclear tests rendered the proceedings pointless, the ICJ took the view that issuing a substantive judgment on the merits of the case would not contribute to the Court's dispute-settlement mission.[33] Indeed, in the latter case, which formally speaking did not involve the invocation of an inherent power to decline jurisdiction, but rather an inherent power to preliminarily address a question of merits having an antecedent character, the Court overtly explained the rationale behind its position:

The Court therefore sees no reason to allow the continuance of proceedings which it knows are bound to be fruitless. While judicial settlement may provide path to international harmony in circumstances of conflict, it is none the less true that the needless continuance of litigation is an obstacle to such harmony.[34]

Arguably, PCIJ/ICJ cases where the Court declined to exercise jurisdiction because they directly implicated the legal rights and interests

[31] *Savu* v. *Romania,* Application no. 29218/05, ECtHR Decision of 11 October 2011, paras 29–30.

[32] *Northern Cameroons* (*Cameroon* v. *UK*), 1963 ICJ 15.

[33] *Nuclear Tests* (*Australia* v. *France*), 1974 ICJ 253.

[34] *Ibid.*, at 271.

of a third party – *Eastern Carelia,*[35] *Monetary Gold*[36] *and East Timor*[37] – also touch on considerations of efficiency. In all these cases, it seems likely that the Court's ability to ascertain fully the facts of the cases without the cooperation of the relevant third parties would have been seriously compromised. As a result, its ability to resolve the dispute, or even to engage in a useful law-application exercise, may have been rendered improbable.

From this perspective, one may view the ICJ's treatment of issues of merits of a preliminary nature, such as lack of standing[38] or failure to exhaust local remedies (when regarded as a substantive part of the legal claim),[39] as an exercise of discretion governed by comparable policy considerations of legitimacy and effectiveness to those governing admissibility decisions. For example, one may understand the position taken by the Court in *South West Africa* as an attempt to extricate the ICJ from a thorny political controversy not linked to any specific interstate dispute, through the invocation of the *actio popularis* doctrine.[40] In the same vein, the consideration in *ELSI* as to whether domestic remedies were exhausted as a preliminary requirement for establishing the responsibility of the host state vis-à-vis the investor and its state of nationality can be viewed as driven by effectiveness considerations. The deployment of international dispute-settlement resources in circumstances in which local authorities have not been afforded every opportunity to resolve the dispute through domestic legal procedures may be costly and unnecessary.

Admissibility as a jurisdiction-regulating measure

The exercise of discretion in the context of the application of admissibility rules may also function as a jurisdiction-regulating mechanism, that is, as a specific case-selection method informed by the

35 *Status of Eastern Carelia,* 1923 PCIJ (Ser B) No 5.

36 *Monetary Gold Removed from Rome in 1943* (*Italy* v. *France et al.*), 1954 ICJ 19.

37 *East Timor* (*Portugal* v. *Australia*), 1995 ICJ 90.

38 *South West Africa,* 1966 ICJ 6; *Nottebohm* (*Liechtenstein* v. *Guatemala*), 1953 ICJ 111; *Barcelona Traction, Light and Power Company, Ltd* (*Belgium* v. *Spain*), 1970 ICJ 3 (second phase).

39 *Elettronica Sicula S.p.A. (ELSI)* (*USA* v. *Italy*), 1989 ICJ 15, 42.

40 One may argue, however, that the decision of the Court not to examine a decolonization related claim did more harm than good to its legitimacy, leading it shortly thereafter to reverse its position and enunciate a broad *erga omnes* doctrine. *Barcelona Traction, Light and Power Company, Ltd* (*Belgium* v. *Spain*), 1970 ICJ 3, 32.

availability of other dispute-settlement or problem-solving forums. I already alluded to the PCIJ's *Minority Schools in Upper Silesia* case as establishing the principle that a forum selection provision found in an international instrument conferring a dispute-settlement procedure with exclusive jurisdiction may lead the Court to decline jurisdiction over a case validly referred to it.[41] This principle may be extended to choice of forum provisions found not only in international instruments, but also in private contracts. Indeed, in the *Vivendi* arbitration, an ICSID tribunal held that a contractual provision bars it from addressing the factual aspect of the dispute, which the parties have agreed to refer to domestic litigation:

> Given the nature of the dispute between Claimants and the Province of Tucumán, it is not possible for this Tribunal to determine which actions of the Province were taken in exercise of its sovereign authority and which in the exercise of its rights as a party to the Concession Contract considering, in particular, that much of the evidence presented in this case has involved detailed issues of performance and rates under the Concession Contract. To make such determinations, the Tribunal would have to undertake a detailed interpretation and application of the Concession Contract, a task left by the parties to that contract to the exclusive jurisdiction of the administrative courts of Tucumán.[42]

Nevertheless, the willingness of international tribunals to decline jurisdiction as part of their jurisdiction-regulating policies appears to be limited, since such a decision may conflict with their dispute-settlement mission and frustrate the expectations of the parties to adjudication. Indeed, in *Vivendi*, an *ad hoc* committee convened at the request of the investor nullified the decision of the arbitration panel, holding, in essence, that the tribunal erred by refusing to exercise jurisdiction because of a contractual compromissory clause. According to the *ad hoc* committee, a private contract between an investor and a host state cannot detract from the substantive claims and procedural

[41] *Minority Schools*, 1928 PCIJ (ser A) No 15, at 22–23.

[42] *Compañiá de Aguas del Aconquija S.A. and Vivendi Universal S.A.* v. *Argentine Republic*, ICSID Case No. ARB/97/3, Award of 21 November 2000, at para 79. For a comparable decision on jurisdiction, see the *Southern Bluefin Tuna* case in which an Annex VII UNCLOS arbitral tribunal took the view that its jurisdiction should be declined in the face of competing jurisdictional arrangements – article 16 of the 1993 Convention for the Conservation of Southern Bluefin Tuna. *Southern Bluefin Tuna* (*Australia* v. *Japan; New Zealand* v. *Japan*), Award on Jurisdiction and Admissibility, Decision of 4 August 2000, 39 ILM (2000) 1359.

rights created by the interstate bilateral investment treaty (BIT).[43] Put differently, the *ad hoc* committee did not agree that the tribunal properly exercised its power to decline jurisdiction under the BIT for the purpose of accommodating a jurisdictional arrangement created by a private contract.

In the same vein, attempts made by the Czech Republic in *Lauder/CME* to reject parallel proceedings brought against it on grounds of the *abus de droit* principle had failed, since both tribunals involved in the parallel proceedings took the view that their power to decline jurisdiction in the face of another legal process ought to be exercised only if the two proceedings are sufficiently similar in nature. For example, the United Nations Commission on International Trade Law (UNCITRAL) tribunal (sitting in Stockholm), before which the investment claim of the Lauder controlled corporation was adjudicated, held that it would retain jurisdiction even if Lauder himself engaged in *abus de droit*:

> Should two different Treaties grant remedies to the respective claimants deriving from the same facts and circumstances, this does not deprive one of the claimants of jurisdiction, if jurisdiction is granted under the respective Treaty. A possible abuse by Mr. Lauder in pursuing his claim under the US Treaty as alleged by the Respondent does not affect jurisdiction in these arbitration proceedings.[44]

At the same time, the United Nations Convention on the Law of the Sea (UNCLOS) and International Centre for the Settlement of Investment Disputes (ICSID) arbitral tribunals adopted a more pro-regulatory approach to competing jurisdictions in *MOX* and *SGS* v. *Philippines*, respectively.[45] In both cases, the existence of legal obligations found in other treaties and contractual provisions regulating jurisdiction over related disputes led the seized tribunals to stay proceedings until the end of the competing proceedings. These

[43] *Compañiá de Aguas del Aconquija S.A. and Vivendi Universal S.A.* v. *Argentine Republic*, ICSID Case No. ARB/97/3, Decision on Annulment of 3 July 2002, at para 103.

[44] *CME Czech Republic B.V.* v. *The Czech Republic*, UNCITRAL Partial Award of 13 September 2001, para. 412, www.italaw.com/sites/default/files/case-documents/ita0178.pdf.

[45] *MOX Plant* (*Ireland* v. *UK*), UNCLOS Annex VII Arbitral Tribunal Order No. 3 of 24 June 2003 (Suspension of Proceedings on Jurisdiction and Merits, and Request For Further Provisional Measures); *SGS Société Générale de Surveillance S.A.* v. *Philippines*, Decision of ICSID Tribunal on Objections to Jurisdiction of 29 January 2004.

decisions, which do not amount to a decline of jurisdiction, illustrate that international tribunals may have inherent powers pertaining to the manner in which they exercise jurisdiction, other than declaring cases which fall inside their jurisdictional ambit as admissible or inadmissible, and that these powers can also be harnessed to serve relevant policy goals, including jurisdiction regulation.

In some cases, the application of jurisdictional conditions serves to regulate jurisdiction in a manner which resembles the specific case selection attributes of admissibility rules. For example, although the requirement to exhaust local remedies is in most cases a jurisdictional condition, delineating the authority bestowed upon an international court (alternatively, it may serve as a substantive condition of international responsibility), it serves as a jurisdiction-regulating rule denying at times jurisdiction from international courts in favour of legal proceedings at the domestic level. International courts do, however, enjoy a degree of discretion in determining whether in a particular case remedies have been exhausted or whether they have been excessively prolonged. For instance, the above-mentioned decision by the ECtHR in *Aksoy* v. *Turkey* to regard the mere interviewing of a torture victim by a prosecutor as sufficient to satisfy the exhaustion requirement functions in practice as an admissibility decision: a case-specific decision to assume jurisdiction over the case.[46]

In all cases where international courts employ rules of admissibility or other decision-making powers entailing a similar case-selection function in order to regulate the allocation of jurisdiction, they may consider policy considerations relating to the choice of adjudication forum. They may choose to refer the dispute to the forum enjoying the strongest form of legal acceptance of jurisdiction (e.g. governed by an exclusive jurisdiction clause); the forum best situated to address the relevant issues of law or fact;[47] or the forum whose

[46] *Aksoy* v. *Turkey*, App. No, 21987/93, 1996-IV EHRR (No. 26), paras 56–57:

> [T]he injuries he had sustained must have been clearly visible during their meeting. However, the prosecutor chose to make no enquiry as to the nature, extent and cause of these injuries, despite the fact that in Turkish law he was under a duty to investigate (see para. 26) ... Having seen that the public prosecutor was aware of his injuries but had taken no action, it is understandable if the applicant formed the belief that he could not hope to secure concern and satisfaction through national legal channels. The Court therefore concludes that there existed special circumstances which absolved the applicant from his obligation to exhaust domestic remedies.

[47] See *SGS* v. *Philippines*, note 45, paras 171–174.

exercise of jurisdiction is consistent with a general principle of international law, such as national sovereignty (which may support, e.g., allowing states to utilize their own courts to remedy any alleged violation of international law before the matter is brought before an international court).[48] Yet, international courts may tend to retain cases even in the face of a competing suitable forum when they have a strong institutional interest in adjudicating them. This may be either because adjudication promotes the systemic welfare of their overarching regime (e.g. the interest that trade disputes between World Trade Organization (WTO) member states be adjudicated at the WTO Dispute Settlement Body (DSB), rather than in regional forums,[49] or that ICSID should not be circumvented in order to promote the protection of investments),[50] or because international courts are keen on preserving their own relevance to the subject matter at hand.

The ICJ case law on preliminary objections brought before it, calling it to decline jurisdiction over disputes of a predominantly political character, is illustrative of the latter type of policy considerations. In several cases, states appearing before the ICJ have claimed that other UN organs – most typically the Security Council – are better suited to handle such disputes.[51] In rejecting these admissibility objections, the Court took the view that the UN Charter does not exclude the exercise of jurisdiction in parallel by the UN judicial and political organs,[52] and that no overriding policy considerations support a decision to decline jurisdiction since the exercise of

48 See e.g. *Interhandel* (Switzerland v. US) 1959 ICJ 6, 27.

49 See e.g. *Mexico – Tax Measures on Soft Drinks and OtherBeverages,* Report of the AB of 6 March 2006, WTO Doc. WT/DS308/AB/R; Argentina – Definitive Anti-Dumping Duties on Poultry from Brazil, Report of the Panel of 22 April 2003, WTO Doc. WT/DS241/R (2003).

50 *Abaclat* v. *Argentina,* ICSID Case No. ARB/07/5, Decision of 4 August 2011, at paras 580–584 (explaining why an 18-month waiting period before moving from national to international adjudication, which is provided for in the BIT, can be disposed of).

51 See e.g., *Military and Paramilitary Activities in Nicaragua* (*Nicaragua* v. *US*), 1984 ICJ at 434–435; *Legal Consequences of the Construction of a Wall in the Occupied Palestinian Territories,* 2004 ICJ 136, 148.

52 See *United States Diplomatic and Consular Staff in Tehran* (*US* v. *Iran*), 1980 ICJ 3, 22:

> Whereas Article 12 of the Charter expressly forbids the General Assembly to make any recommendation with regard to a dispute or situation while the Security Council is exercising its functions in respect of that dispute or situation, no such restriction is placed on the functioning of the Court by any provision of either the Charter or the Statute of the Court.

judicial and political authority is complementary in nature.[53] While the ICJ has been criticized for facilitating the politicization of its proceedings through a timid application of its powers to decline jurisdiction,[54] one may speculate that part of the reasons for the Court's approach is its institutional interest in retaining relevance in high-profile conflicts implicating international peace and security, and to strengthen the previously marginalized role of international law in such conflicts.

[53] *Military and Paramilitary Activities in Nicaragua* (*Nicaragua* v. *US*), 1984 ICJ at 435; *Legal Consequences of the Construction of a Wall in the Occupied Palestinian Territories,* 2004 ICJ 136, 160.

[54] See e.g. Ruth Mackenzie *et al.* (eds.), *Manual on International Courts and Tribunals* 2nd edn. (New York: Oxford University Press, 2010), pp. 36–37; Franklin Berman, 'The International Court of Justice as an Agent of Legal Development?', in Christian J Tams and James Sloan (eds.), *The Development of International Law by the International Court of Justice* (New York: Oxford University Press, 2013), p. 15.

Conclusions

Conferral of jurisdiction implies the empowerment of international courts by their mandate providers and the parties to adjudication, while jurisdictional conditions denote constraints on the adjudicative power that was delegated. Still, the relations between jurisdictional authorizations and conditions are hardly those between a rule and an exception. Since there is no background presumption of jurisdictional competence in international law, international courts only have the jurisdictional power that was actually delegated to them, and may exercise jurisdiction only with regard to those states (or other actors related to those states) that have accepted their jurisdiction. Such acts of delegation and consent are delineated both by positive formulations describing the transactions subject to the court's jurisdiction and by negative formulations describing the transactions not subject to its jurisdiction. Thus, the International Court of Justice (ICJ) was correct, I believe, in refusing to embrace a canon of interpretation narrowly construing exceptions to jurisdiction even when dealing with reservations to declarations of jurisdictional acceptance.[1]

Admissibility rules, in the manner I propose to construe them, differ from jurisdictional conditions. They do not delineate the conferral of jurisdiction on international courts, but rather define the circumstances in which they may decline jurisdiction. Hence, they are exceptional in nature: parties to adjudication, and at times international courts themselves, may invoke them as justifications for decisions not to exercise the adjudicative powers conferred upon

[1] See e.g. *Fisheries Jurisdiction* (*Spain* v. *Canada*), 1998 ICJ 432, 453.

them, notwithstanding the expectations of some or even all of the parties to the case.

Viewed in this light, the traditional categories for discussing the jurisdiction of international courts – jurisdiction *ratione personae, ratione materiae, ratione temporis* and *ratione loci* – may sometimes seem to serve little purpose, except perhaps as useful points of reference for textbook writers. Thus, this book offers an alternative typology, which may inform us about international courts' source of authority, the burden of proof attendant to different terms and conditions, the procedural stages in which they would normally be considered and the scope of discretion accompanying their application. This typology includes a distinction between foundational jurisdiction and the general conditions attached thereto, specific jurisdiction and the specific conditions attached to it, issues of admissibility (divided into terms and conditions emanating from the jurisdiction-conferring instruments, inherent powers and other international undertakings of the adjudicating parties) and questions of merits of a preliminary nature. Understanding the exercise of jurisdiction as a multi-layered process of decision-making helps in drawing attention to hierarchical and interpretative relations between different sources of authority originating from different actors and normative sources. Still, I must acknowledge that the proposed typology does not fully obviate the need to engage in some hair splitting between different aspects of what are essentially intertwined jurisdictional issues.

Decisions on jurisdiction and admissibility are ultimately decisions about case selection: Jurisdictional decisions essentially address a category-based case selection, while admissibility decisions entail specific case selection. One may also note that jurisdictional decisions tend to be based on the interpretation and application of pre-existing case-selection choices made by the mandate providers and the adjudicating parties, whereas admissibility decisions often involve the exercise of discretion by the relevant international court as to what would be judicially proper. There is little question that, in both sets of decisions, policy considerations take pride of place, and that international courts weigh a host of considerations pertaining to their own legitimacy and effectiveness, as well as to the legitimacy and effectiveness of the overarching legal regime or regimes in which they operate.

In practice, though, the differences between jurisdiction and admissibility may be smaller than expected. The interpretation of jurisdictional authorizations and conditions is sometimes performed with a view to specific case-selection considerations, and the application of such general standards has been at times rather selective in nature. At the same time, the expectation that similar cases will be treated alike has led over time to the consolidation of rules on the exercise of discretion in admissibility decisions, rendering them, in essence, tools for category-based case selection.

Hopefully, a better understanding of the options and choices presented to international judges when deciding whether to exercise adjudicative power will render this important process of international governance more transparent and will ensure that international judges are more accountable. I also hope that encouraging international lawyers and judges to think about jurisdiction and admissibility as policy tools, with distinct analytical and procedural attributes, will facilitate their utilization in a manner conducive to promoting the legitimacy and effectiveness of international courts and the international legal system – at least to the extent that they are interested in advancing the project of international governance and the international rule of law as currently configured.

Author index

Author index

Subject index

For EU product safety concerns, contact us at Calle de José Abascal, 56–1°,
28003 Madrid, Spain or eugpsr@cambridge.org.

www.ingramcontent.com/pod-product-compliance
Lightning Source LLC
LaVergne TN
LVHW011520200926
848484LV00001B/91
* 9 7 8 1 1 0 7 0 3 8 7 9 0 *